perfectly I'Mperfect

remarkable stories of
ordinary women overcoming
extraordinary circumstances

COMPILED BY
Nina DeAngelo & Tara Hurst

Perfectly I'Mperfect
remarkable stories of ordinary women overcoming extraordinary circumstances
Two Chicks & A Dream Publishing, LLC

Published by Two Chicks & A Dream Publishing, LLC, O'Fallon, MO
Copyright ©2023
All rights reserved.

No part of this publication may be reproduced, stored in a retrieval system, or transmitted in any form or by any means, electronic, mechanical, photocopying, recording, scanning, or otherwise, except as permitted under Section 107 or 108 of the 1976 United States Copyright Act, without the prior written permission of the Publisher. Requests to the Publisher for permission should be addressed to nina@dynamicshiftconsulting.com, please put Perfectly I'Mperfect in the subject line.

Limit of Liability/Disclaimer of Warranty: While the publisher and author have used their best efforts in preparing this book, they make no representations or warranties with respect to the accuracy or completeness of the contents of this book and specifically disclaim any implied warranties of merchantability or fitness for a particular purpose. No warranty may be created or extended by sales representatives or written sales materials. The advice and strategies contained herein may not be suitable for your situation. You should consult with a professional where appropriate. Neither the publisher nor author shall be liable for any loss of profit or any other commercial damages, including but not limited to special, incidental, consequential, or other damages.

All contributing authors to this anthology have submitted their chapters to an editing process, and have accepted the recommendations of the editors at their own discretion. All authors have approved their chapters prior to publication.

Cover, Interior Design, and Project Management:
  Davis Creative Publishing, DavisCreativePublishing.com

Writing Coach and Editor: L. Carol Scott

Compilation by Nina DeAngelo and Tara Hurst

Library of Congress Cataloging-in-Publication Data
(Provided by Cassidy Cataloguing Services, Inc.)

Names: DeAngelo, Nina, compiler. | Hurst, Tara, compiler.
Title: Perfectly I'Mperfect : remarkable stories of ordinary women overcoming extraordinary circumstances / compiled by Nina DeAngelo & Tara Hurst.
Other titles: Perfectly imperfect
Description: O'Fallon, MO : Two Chicks & A Dream Publishing, LLC, [2023] | Includes bibliographical references.
Identifiers: ISBN: 979-8-9889477-0-7 (paperback) | 979-8-9889477-1-4 (ebook) | LCCN: 2023917927
Subjects: LCSH: Self-esteem in women. | Imperfection--Psychological aspects. | Motivation (Psychology) | Resilience (Personality trait) | Self-talk. | Life change events--Psychological aspects. | Courage. | LCGFT: Self-help publications. | BISAC: SELF HELP / Motivational & Inspirational. | BODY, MIND & SPIRIT / Inspiration & Personal Growth. | SELF HELP / Personal Growth/Success.
Classification: LCC: BF697.5.S46 P47 2023 | DDC: 158.1--dc23

TRIGGER WARNING:
Several chapters in this book describe the authors' experiences overcoming the effects of violence—including childhood sexual assault and marital abuse, self-harm and suicide—as well as less-than-positive coping strategies for the resulting trauma, such as sexual acting out and overuse of alcohol and both prescribed and illegal street drugs.

We have identified these chapters with a DAISY ✿ to empower reader's choice.

TABLE OF CONTENTS

Cathy Davis | Foreword vi
Nina DeAngelo | Unleashing the Brave Within:
    Embracing the Power of Courage 1
Tara Hurst | The Other Side of Fear and Doubt 7
Tammy Egelhoff | Heal the Wound, But Leave the Scar. 13
Teresa Reiniger | Finding Purpose at Sixty. 20
Dr. Alanna McNelly | Now I Know 26
Ann Bender | Living Thru Death's Eyes ✿. 32
Danielle Solito | Look Up. 38
Sequoia Haskell | All Masters Were Once Disasters 44
Nicole Tucker | Shattering the Mask ✿. 51
Jan Kraus | Once Upon a Friendship. 57
Jaqueline Larrecou-Whipple | A Journey of Hope ✿ 63
Jenny Gaume | Aren't You Embarrassed?. 69
Jess Beeson | Damn It! I Forgot My Bra! 75
Jessica Grace | Self-Love: The Simplest Solution 81
Kathryn Malloy | You Are Stronger Than You Seem ✿ 87
Katie Fry | She Believed She Could…So She Did 93
Laura DeVries | What Is Your Aha! Moment? 99
Lynn Baribault | Am I Really Enough as I Am Now?. 105
Megan Rieke | And Then There Was Joy ✿. 111
Nancy Thompson | Borrowed Confidence 117

Natalie Taylor-Levin | The Best Is Yet to Come ✿ 123

Pamela Fenili | Cracks in the Crystal Ball ✿. 129

Nicole Gaither | Shift Happens ✿ 135

Tabatha Baker | God's Timing 141

Paula Bubb Whiting | Growing Through What We Go Through ✿ . . 147

Heather L. Kemper | From Shadows to Self-Love:
    Owning Your Story ✿ 153

Deanna Rose | Then the Miracle ✿ 160

Pooja Arshanapally | The Strength in Silence. 167

Rachel Boone | Rekindle Your Spark. 173

Rose Perry | Light Is Coming ✿ 179

Sara Chandler | The Grace Period ✿. 185

Sarah Lowe | Plan B. 191

Shashanna Davis | Sisu (SEE-soo) ✿. 197

Shelly Clark | Wins Aren't Always Determined by a Score 203

Tonya Steinmeyer and Keri Szwarc | All for a Reason 209

Tracee White | No Isn't a Bad Word 216

Stephanie Malench | From Under the Thumb to
    Large and In Charge 221

Terri Schneider | New Beginnings ✿ 227

Tonya Winingar | How the Hell Did I Do THAT? 233

Traci S. Daniels | The Gift That Keeps on Giving... 239

Wendy Edelstein | Home Owned 245

Acknowledgements. 251

Cathy Davis

Foreword

On the short list of what many people feel they lost most during the pandemic, you'll inevitably find HOPE and a sense of COMMUNITY near the top. For some, navigating a post-pandemic world alone can be like walking blindfolded without a guide—you are never really sure what you might encounter.

Several years ago (at least a dozen or so), I was taking a workshop at a retreat center and one of our exercises was a Trust Walk. We were asked to pair up with one other person and wait for further instructions.
1. Our first step was for one of us to volunteer to close our eyes and let the other guide us around the retreat center and its immediate outdoor garden. The rules included no conversation—only for the open-eyed person to gently nudge and guide with their hand to keep the closed-eye participant safe and out of harm.
2. The second step was to change roles at the sound of a bell.

There had to have been at least 10 sets of two people each wandering about during the exercise. I had my eyes closed and I could feel the hand of my "buddy" on my shoulder, gently maneuvering me, at a slow pace, inside the building and eventually out into the garden area. We had been walking for about 10 minutes when I heard the voice of the facilitator in front of me, gently asking, "Excuse me for interrupting, ladies…but can either of you tell me just exactly who is guiding, and who is walking with your eyes closed?!"

You see, BOTH of us had been taking our Trust Walk with our eyes closed—at the same time! The amazing part is that we never bumped into walls, furniture, trees, nor even other people. The power of the community kicked in and those around us moved out of our way. In addition, our 6th sense (some say our third eye) kicked in and helped us avoid stumbling over inanimate objects or tripping on steps—all the while keeping us out of harm's way.

This concept of navigating through the help of our community can also be seen with flocks of geese. Geese use the concept of community to succeed in getting the flock to its final destination.

- **FACT:** Geese fly in a "V" formation, increasing their flight range by 71% (versus flying solo).

- **FOOD-FOR-THOUGHT:** People who share a common direction and a sense of community get where they are going more quickly and easily when traveling on the trust of one another.

- **FACT:** When the front goose gets tired, she rotates back in the wing and another goose steps up to fly as the leader.

- **FOOD-FOR-THOUGHT:** It pays to take turns doing hard jobs and trust that we can rely upon others to step in when we need them.

- **FACT:** Whenever a goose falls out of formation, it feels the drag and resistance of trying to go it alone, and quickly gets back into formation to take advantage of the lifting power of the flock.

- **FOOD-FOR-THOUGHT:** If we have as much sense as a goose, we'll stay in alignment with those who are headed in the same positive direction that we are.

- **FACT:** Geese honk as they fly, encouraging those up front to keep up their speed.
- **FOOD-FOR-THOUGHT:** We need to be careful what we say when we honk from behind. Better to be the "cheerleader" rather than the "fear-leader".

(Brings about a whole new meaning to "getting goosed!")

The power of community is alive and well in *"Perfectly I'Mperfect!"*

Nina, Tara, Carol, Julie, and I have watched these aspiring authors step into their power and be willing to share their words of wisdom to change the world for the better. Little did we know the powerful stories these women were ready to bring forth while offering HOPE and COMMUNITY to others!

I applaud and honor the perseverance and bravery I've seen brought forward as this group of women dug deep and "birthed" their words of wisdom—each showing a willingness to STEP UP, STAND UP, and LIFT UP each other!

May these words inspire and lift you to new heights, too!

Nina DeAngelo

Unleashing the Brave Within: Embracing the Power of Courage

I couldn't believe what I had just heard. As I took in the incredible news, my heart swelled with love and admiration—emotions I had never before felt toward myself. I wasn't sure what to do with these newfound feelings.

We all have courage deep within us. If we have the desire and ability to tap into it, that can propel us forward. From the meekest to the most gallant, we all possess the capacity to gather our inner strength and face life's challenges.

But what is courage, exactly? Courage is not the absence of fear, but rather the ability to act despite fear. It is a willingness to step outside our comfort zones, take risks, and confront our fears and doubts. Courage can be cultivated and nurtured, allowing us to tap into our true potential. All we need is positive thinking, self-belief, and resilience.

These three skills, together, form the foundation for courage. The power of positive thinking is a real thing and literally rewires your brain with programming to better serve you. Self-belief propels you into areas of your life you never thought possible. Resilience keeps you standing back up after being knocked down and brings you the ability to move forward regardless of the obstacles in your way.

Something snapped!

When I was eighteen years old, I knew I wanted a better hand of cards for the game of life than the one I was dealt. I was raised in a family with an alcoholic, gambling father and an emotionally unavailable mother. Not an environment that instilled a lot of positive thinking or self-belief but was, perhaps, the awakening of my resilience. At the ripe young age of eighteen, I decided my best bet for making something for myself was to join the Army and leave my hometown of Alton, Illinois. So, three months after graduating high school in 1991, I enlisted. Can you guess my family's and my friends' first reactions when I told them what I had done? They said things like, "You'll never make it, you're too weak, you're too cute, you're too short, you're too girly." And the list of reasons why I wouldn't be successful as a soldier went on and on. What kind of mindset do you think I took with me into basic training? If you guessed negative self-talk and self-doubt, you're completely right.

Let me set the stage for you. When I went through basic training, it was still a man's Army. I had all male drill sergeants. They were rough and tough, and they offered no lighter hand with us ladies who had just signed our name on the dotted line. I remember one in particular, Drill Sergeant Montgomery. He fixated on me from the minute I stepped off that bus at basic training. A very tall man, he was easily six feet, if not taller. I'm just five feet, even on a good day with my hair fixed! As I stood in formation, Drill Sergeant Montgomery walked around me, repeatedly "shoulder-checking" me—that is, using his shoulder to hit me with force and aggression—and shoving his face up close to mine. He said things like, "You think you got what it takes to make it in my Army, private?" and "Well, well, aren't you the pretty, petite one?"

I was scared to death! All the negative comments from my family and friends still swirled around inside my head. The thought that I had made the biggest mistake in my life crossed my mind several times. I was shaking on the inside and felt my belly swell with fear, certain I would throw up from the stress from this "exchange of pleasantries." But then something happened.

Something snapped within me. I stood firmly in place and told myself, *this man gets paid to break me down so he can build me up to be a successful soldier*. And I stood there, withstanding his abuse without showing one bit of emotion. *That* was a new reaction for me! Previously, confrontations with much less aggression than that would have sent me running and crying. This moment was the first step of my journey into positive self-talk, self-belief, and resilience.

You are what you speak, and what you think!

For the duration of my time in basic training, Drill Sergeant Montgomery continued to pick on me, tell me how weak I was, and berate me at every opportunity. He even took me and several of my bunkmates into our classroom to exercise for hours at a time. I remember one instance vividly. I was yanked from sleep in my bunk by bright lights and Drill Sergeant Montgomery yelling and screaming for me and my bunkmates to get up and be in the classroom in five minutes, full canteen in hand. As we appeared, each of us was also handed a dummy weapon—a life-size replica of an M16 rifle but made of rubber. And they are heavy. We did hours and hours of exercises, jumping jacks, mountain climbers, sit-ups, push-ups, and more, until the walls in the classroom were sweating!

I chanted my reminder, in the safety of my own head, that he was getting paid to break me down so he could build me up to be a successful soldier. Several of my bunkmates were falling from exhaustion and heat stress. As each one fell out of formation, I repeated more positive self-talk to keep going. I told myself things like "you can do this" and "you are a goddess warrior, and you will not give him the satisfaction of breaking you." I stood tall—well, as tall as I could at five feet—and endured all his torture until even *he* was exhausted. Then I knew the secret: I had loved myself through this and would find all the positive self-talk I needed to muster until I graduated.

I think I can, I think I can!

Drill Sergeant Montgomery was on me to study for all of my tests, and if he caught me without my study guide in hand, I would do push-ups until he was tired! After weeks and weeks of studying, it was time. My tests included skills such as disassembling my M16 and properly putting it back together within a certain timeframe, donning my hazmat suit, administering first aid to my battle buddy, being able to properly communicate a message over the hand radio, and much, much more.

I was so nervous as I approached each testing station. Then, one by one, I passed each task presented. After the first few stations, I started to believe in myself! In fact, I *knew* I was going to pass these tests with flying colors, and—you know what?—I did! I spoke my fervently positive self-talk into the Universe, and I made it happen.

Not only did I receive a 100 percent score on each test, but I was also handpicked to go before a panel of highly ranked non-commissioned officers—all Sergeant Majors, to be exact—and respond to their questions on the rules of engagement during wartime, the Geneva convention, and many other administrative-type questions. I could not demonstrate any of my practiced skills for the panel, but all the knowledge they tested was part of the study guide. I was a nervous wreck. Not only was I expected to answer each question correctly, but I was also expected to remember to address each Sergeant Major correctly with each answer I gave.

I wasn't the only private selected for this level of examination, but I'm happy to report I shone, only missing one question. Wow, I thought, I really can do this! One thing I did notice as I was waiting to go in and answer questions from this panel of highly decorated non-commission officers was that there were other privates also waiting. I found this to be a bit peculiar; however, I truly didn't give it much thought after seeing others coming out of that room. I just wondered what was in store for me.

I'm sorry…what?!

After all of the tests and questions and back in the barracks, I heard Drill Sergeant Montgomery yelling for me from his office down the hall. You better believe I ran as quickly as I could to arrive at his feet as fast as I could. Once I was in front of him, he made me drop and give him the by-now-expected push-ups. Inviting me to sit down, he proceeded to tell me that ever since I stepped foot off that bus on day one of basic training, he saw something in me, something he felt confident he could nurture.

I learned that all of the competitions I had just completed included the goal of designating a prestigious honor: Solider of the Cycle. Drill Sergeant Montgomery told me I had been chosen as the top private among six hundred graduating soldiers! I was dumbfounded, and I finally understood that this mentor had been grooming me to graduate at the top of my basic training Brigade, all along.

So, there we are, at that moment when my heart swelled with love and admiration…and for the first time those emotions were fully directed toward myself. And so I did: I graduated with top honors, was recognized at graduation, and was grateful to walk in a special procession in recognition of my achievement. I owe so much to Drill Sergeant Montgomery. Because of him and his ability to sense something in me that I didn't even sense in myself, I learned the power of positive thinking, I gained a *ton* of self-belief, and now I truly understand the meaning of resilience.

So, remember, courage is not reserved for the lucky; it is a universal trait that lives in all of us. It is a force that can propel us toward personal growth, achievement, and fulfillment. May you embark on many adventures in your lifetime that help you discover boundless courage!

Nina DeAngelo is a highly skilled Neuro-Linguistics Programming (NLP) master coach and trainer, and an empowerment speaker. With years of experience in the field, Nina has honed her expertise in NLP to empower individuals and teams to reach their full potential. Through her dynamic coaching and training sessions, she has helped hundreds of individuals unlock their inner strengths, overcome obstacles, and achieve personal and professional success. As an engaging and inspiring speaker, Nina captivates audiences with her motivating messages of self-empowerment, resilience, and personal growth. She is known for her warm, friendly approach, which creates a safe and supportive environment for growth and transformation. Aspiring leaders in corporations and nonprofits seek out Nina as a coach and teacher for both personal and professional development. As her passion unlocks their true potential, they find greater purpose and fulfillment in their lives. Nina's passion for helping others shines in every interaction and makes her a sought-after coach, trainer, and speaker in the field of personal and professional development as she guides individuals to unlock their true potential and live a life of purpose and fulfillment.

Tara Hurst

The Other Side of Fear and Doubt

The universe whispers to us our entire lives…until it doesn't. If you go long enough without listening to it, it no longer whispers. It begins with a gentle nudge, then moves to a friendly push, then to a hard shove. And if you still aren't listening, a slap in the face that wakes you right up. That final slap can shake you to your core; you feel it in your soul.

When I began my journey to health a decade ago, I thought my life would change drastically if I just lost some weight and did more self-care, like getting pedicures and massages. So I did those things, and even lost more than one hundred pounds. Yet I still wasn't completely healthy or free from my own internal mind games. I still had the same negative self-talk, the same self-sabotaging behaviors, and the same lack of belief in myself that had been with me for as long as I could remember. I had released the fat that my body had stored from years of not loving myself enough. I just couldn't shed the weight of the world or the weight of whatever in own mind was holding me down. I was the mountain I couldn't seem to climb.

I finally made a decision that has changed my life and led me here. It was time that I got out of my comfort zone, owned my own s#!t, and finally accepted the fact that I had been the obstacle the entire time. I was the one standing in my way from the beginning. For the first time in my life, I took a hard look at myself and accepted responsibility for who

I was and where I was. I let go of the guilt, shame, and disappointment that I had been carrying around for years. This major transformation began with the realization that I had done the best I could at the time with the tools I had.

And that is when the universe started trying to get my attention. First the nudge, then the friendly shove…

The Nudge

I had thought about health coaching but always found multiple excuses why I would never be successful. Then, when the pandemic hit, my husband was left without either of his two incomes. So I took a leap of faith and began health coaching to supplement our family income. What started as leading a few friends on their journeys has led me to an opportunity to give hope, inspiration, and motivation to countless others, all while keeping myself accountable.

Not long after the nudge, the universe felt I was ready for a little friendly shove…pushing me out of my comfort zones and into new situations. Health coaching posed opportunities and raised responsibilities that required me to face my biggest fears. If I wanted change, I was going to have to be the force for that change.

Next came that hard shove. I was still working as a full-time child care director, which was crushing my soul. I was building up my coaching business in my spare time. Also working on opening a record store with my husband and running a household, I was mentally and emotionally drained. Still, I was committed to succeeding at everything.

Just in time, I discovered daily affirmations. Those little sentences, awkward at first, were crazy powerful and quickly became the source of my superpower! I am strong. I am capable. I am enough. And I am a badass who can do hard things! After sixteen years of soul crushing, I turned in my resignation.

In January 2022 the universe delivered what felt like the wake-up slap of all slaps. I decided to go ahead with a total knee replacement but soon realized that something was very wrong. My recovery was too slow, and I was still in constant pain. The most challenging year of my life was about to begin.

When my entire life as I knew it halted, I felt completely unprepared for the mental, emotional, physical, or spiritual impacts. I was in a place where nothing made sense, and I was slowly losing my footing. The longest and most intense battle I had ever faced went on for six months. Constant pain and discomfort combined with sleep issues were taking their toll and getting the best of me. I had never felt so isolated and alone. I had never been so mentally and physically defeated. And I had never had to face the darkness that almost took me down, and so I prayed. I prayed for wisdom, I prayed for guidance, and I prayed for clarity.

Then an *Aha! moment* happened. I realized I wasn't having a breakdown; I was having a breakthrough! I knew I was the answer as much as I was the problem. The nudge, the friendly push…all had led me to this point. Now the universe was ready to show me how to better use the tools I'd had all along.

So what changed? I began praying for guidance rather than praying for purpose, and my faith grew stronger and stronger with every obstacle. Something incredible happened after that knee surgery. I realized I had been "training" for this moment for years.

Not only did I allow myself the opportunity to use the tools in my original toolbox, such as prayer and daily affirmations, but the last tool I picked up proved to be a key to a whole new toolbox. I simply had to have faith that I would discover how to use its contents.

Once I finally understood that nothing happens *to* me, and everything is happening *for* me, I realized that my desire to change was stronger than my desire to stay the same.

That realization required me to sort through the mud and muck of a traumatic childhood; revisit other periods of my life that were overflowing with guilt, shame, and embarrassment; and dig more deeply into my current life, overrun until recently with self-doubt and feelings of inadequacy. So I opened my new toolbox and got to work on me...from the inside out. And here is what happened when I did:

- I heard a call to return to church.
- A desire to serve led me to volunteer.
- A colleague invited me into a new networking group.
- An opportunity to join a women's support group came my way.
- I found my way to a mindset certification program.
- I began to practice meditation.
- I learned to listen.
- I desired change.

As I actively pursued my purpose, I noticed that my doubts were leaving me. I was moving toward dreams that required massive action and tackling challenging goals far outside my comfort zone.

But what had gotten me to this point wasn't going to get me where I needed to be. It was time for new tools:

- I showed up as my authentic self.
- I asked for help.
- I challenged myself.
- I become bold, brave, and unapologetic.
- I lived my life out loud.
- I surrounded myself with hope dealers.

I am now fully committed to my daily routine. I am in love with the realization that I haven't yet met the best version of myself. I focus on daily affirmations and gratitude. I focus on what I want and no longer worry about what I don't. I invest my energy to build a future in which I inspire and influence others. I am committed to strengthening all the relationships in my life, beginning with the one I have with myself.

I began by creating a couple of lists. I identified three items to move closer to my health and wellness goals, and three things to stop doing, which had been holding me back. What quickly became apparent was that I may have been the mountain blocking my path, but I also am one heck of a trail guide! I was learning to be confident by getting out of my own way, and by *doing things while scared*. Who would be better to lead this expedition than the person who raised the mountain in the first place?

So here I am, a driving force behind my first book endeavor and planning my first women's conference. I'm running on caffeine, Jesus, and a whole lot of intuition and grit. I am certainly not the same person I was, but I love and respect her just the same. The day I said, "Alright, Lord, what are we going to do today? Who are we going to inspire? Whose life are we going to change?" transformed me.

For the first time in my life, I feel whole. My cup is full: of hope, love, empathy, and joy. One day, I will be completely open about the life details that almost broke me, but for now I focus my energy on you. I want you to realize that *you* are worth the journey, and that *you* already have the tools to achieve your passion and purpose.

Just open your toolbox. Start treating yourself with the same compassion and encouragement you would offer your child or best friend. To show up for others, start by showing up for yourself. You weren't created to be mediocre. You were meant to do great things, but none of them is meant to be done alone. Do the work, dig deep, grab that coffee, find your superpower, and take a leap of faith.

The truth is this: Everything you desire in this life is on the other side of fear and doubt.

Perfectly I'Mperfect

Tara Hurst is an empowerment and transformational coach who specializes in the realm of health and fitness, energy and spirituality, advancement in business, and love and relationships, focusing on mindfulness and inner chatter. Tara is Neurolinguistic Programming Practitioner, business mentor, public speaker, and a bestselling author. After releasing one hundred pounds a decade ago and beginning her own personal healing journey, Tara began coaching others and empowering them to transform themselves by incorporating the necessary daily habits to ultimately improve their emotional, mental, spiritual, as well as physical well-being. Tara works one-on-one with others to motivate, encourage, and support them, while empowering them to build self-confidence to set new goals and seek growth in every aspect of their lives.

Tammy Egelhoff

Heal the Wound, But Leave the Scar

Kim? KIM! WHERE is my phone!

I need an ambulance right away. I have an unconscious fifty-five-year-old female in my home!

Ma'am, in your home? What is your address? Is she breathing? Does she have a pulse or are there any signs of life?

Pushing through the tears, the fear, the traumatic mental torment… Kim, don't you dare leave me!

Ma'am, I NEED an ambulance right now!

You'll need to move her out of the recliner onto the floor; the ambulance looks to be forty-five minutes out, and you're going to need to start CPR.

Kim, please don't do this. Kim, I love you, I need you!

Ma'am, she won't survive that long! Do you know CPR or will you need assistance?

NO, you don't understand! She just had open heart surgery a week ago and she's in a lot of pain; there's a wound vac in place. How am I supposed to give CPR without hurting or injuring her?

The shock setting in, my voice now quavering…

Ma'am, you must start compressions if you want to save her.

With every chest compression, every breath, I prayed: Kim, stay with me! AND PLEASE, DEAR GOD, where are the paramedics??

My big sister, Kim, boldly stared down life challenges from the moment she was born with a congenital heart defect. As a first grader, she returned to school after open heart surgery bearing a large "T" incision scar on her chest, forever marking the life-altering occasion and generating incessant questions. Strong doesn't even begin to describe her.

I always admired her fortitude and her undeniable free, rebellious spirit. She carried the weight of the universe on her shoulders and somehow made it look like a pair of wings. Choosing to continue to love despite the hurt, heartache, and betrayal life threw her way, she made broken look beautiful and strong look invincible. Yet somehow she thought I was the strong one.

Kim's altruistic path began at an early age as she rescued animals in need of food and love. In time, that desire to love the unlovable grew to include people with broken souls. She was what we call *a natural* in her ability to not only perceive but empathize with the fear and vulnerabilities of others. She stood tall for the underdogs of this world as a strong advocate against injustices toward those who are discarded and forgotten by society.

As sisters, we were as opposite as the sun and moon, but even through conflict we always had each other's backs. Our life experiences had brought us full circle—back home—and we had become reliant upon the trusted oath of sisterhood formed in childhood. We'll always fight, but we'll always make up.

That's what sisters do: we argue, we point out each other's frailties, mistakes, and bad judgment; we flash the insecurities we've had since childhood; and then we come back together. We were each other's strongest allies because I needed her, same as she needed me. Ours was a sisterhood born of blood and tested by fire.

Ma'am, please take as much time as you need with your sister. A new medico voice, in the hospital now, coaching me. Standing guard outside the door, I was still fully committed to the oath between me and my big sister. Then, I finally reached to hold her hand one last time, dreading the final goodbye.

Profound guilt, denial, depression, and a sense of helplessness quickly set in. Emotionally shutting down, withdrawing from life because nothing could repair the artery that had ruptured within my soul. Raised in an environment that taught independence—to be strong and rely upon yourself, not to need or ask anyone for help—we two sisters operated from a lifelong script. We always showed up and showered others with grace, but somehow I couldn't allow that for myself.

Losing my big sister, Kim, was the force that propelled me to turn devastating loss into resilient grief. Drowning in guilt, I believed I had failed that solemn bond to support and protect her. I hadn't saved her in the crucial test. Living with this grief and guilt produced the courage to look deep within.

There I suddenly saw painfully distorted filters limiting my view. I took a sledgehammer to the tall walls of self-reliance I had built without conscious intent and released a voice that spoke of long-held hurts and untold truths. Looking at the past images of that little girl, teen, and woman I once was, who had all become strangers, I clearly saw for the first time the emotionally mangled woman within. I finally understood how the slow but sure poisoning of her soul had taken place.

So, do I now stop, give up, and let go, now that she is "gone?" She was counting on me; she entrusted me with her life. God, you don't understand, she had plans, a future, a lot of life yet to live, and I still need her! *No, I'm afraid you are the one who doesn't understand, my child.*

Heart shattered, lifelong embedded threads separating and disintegrating day by day. The fierce emotions of loss, heartache, and regret were taking a strong hold. I was a ship lost at sea with a broken engine, shattered rudder, and a malfunctioning compass. Rock bottom lay dead ahead, but I couldn't hear what God, Kim, or the universe was trying to say. As a survivor of verbal, mental, religious, and sexual abuse, I had created all those limiting filters and impenetrable walls. What was once a vibrant, loving, and trusting young lady switched to a closed off and guarded individual. The dive deep within to build a new world there soon followed and changed my life. I heard God again: *My child, you thought this was in your hands, in your control?*

Dear God, you graciously spared my mother's life five months ago, yet you refused to show any mercy for my sister? How much broken is enough, God? God, I lay my brokenness at your feet. I cannot embrace your love or understand your purpose, and I need you to heal this wound. You said you'd never leave me, you'd always be my guide, but the storms of life sometimes won't let the sunshine through. Lord, I need to feel that kind of love that only comes from you.

The signs, truths, messages, and three a.m. wake-up calls, God's whispers became louder, clearer. *My child, your hands were to care for, to comfort, to love, but never to carry. Your heart keeps yearning for the love, yet you keep turning away. Take the armor off, set down the shield, and allow yourself to accept not only my grace but the unconditional love that I have always had for you.*

The dark, cold winter months, awaiting the *why* had finally ended; the autopsy report was complete. Emotions raging, I read the bone-chilling words that vividly told the story of a stressed, worn-out heart taking the brutal beatings of life and mustering its final beat that dreadful Christmas day.

Time to stop running from the deafening silence, face the pain and the fear, and free the grip of the demons sent long ago to enslave me. The inner child had been fluttering her tiny wings, desperately trying to free herself. Still in the cold, harsh grip of deep-rooted trauma inflicted by those I had trusted, those whose touch had left a mangled mess, I found courage. Kim's death seemed to lead me into my depths to face the pain there, but it was really to show me the compassionate hand of a stranger sent by Kim. That deep internal dive to face what I had survived also showed me the courage it had taken, courage I needed now to accept Kim's gift to help, restore, and set me free.

For me, acceptance of Kim's death, my past traumas, and God's guidance brought a new chapter, taking back my life and my health. After a lifetime of showing up for everyone else but never myself, I recognized the bad habits and repeated patterns that kept me unhealthy. The result was the release of more than sixty-five pounds of physical weight in five months. With that change came the revelation that we cannot obtain complete health without wellness because it is a packaged deal. Face-to-face with unleashed demons, I embraced the difficult work of inviting the inner child to take a seat, remain present, and voice what she needed in a safe haven. And together we unpacked decades of mental, emotional, and spiritual baggage.

No doubt, God, the universe, and my big sister, Kim, had set this journey in motion. Her death led to my unraveling, an awakening, and invaluable life lessons. Nothing about my recovery from grief and guilt was coincidental—not the journey, the paths, or the strangers along the way. I have observed that many others carry doubts of not being able to cross the distance to their wholeness. I carried those doubts too. And I believe that one courageous step of faith will guide anyone in finding their truth, their authentic self. The secret is to trust the journey, opening ourselves to the strangers found along the path, knowing they are placed there for our good. God, our loved ones who have gone before, and the universe are waiting to love, help, and support us all on these journeys that turn our wounds to scars.

Even in death, Kim kept her oath. She will always be here for me, standing tall within my new circle of chosen sisters. Kim's last post on social media read, "I have a road to find to cross the bridge to better health." Although Kim never got the chance to walk the road to wellness, she sent me on a journey to the precious gift of wholeness.

May our scars always remind us that beauty does exist, even in suffering.

Tammy Egelhoff | Heal the Wound, But Leave the Scar

Tammy Egelhoff is a determined, fiercely independent woman who made the bold decision to walk back into the pits of hell to go get the little girl no one else was coming back for. She went from surviving to thriving by living life with intention, purpose, and gratitude. Tammy is a self-healer and a powerful alchemist who turns pain into power, wounds into wisdom, mistreatment into boundaries, and generational curses into blessings. A loving daughter, sister, wife, mother, and grandmother, she is very passionate about music. Tammy dedicates her chapter to the memory of her sister, Kim Leann Bader.

Teresa Reiniger

Finding Purpose at Sixty

At age eighteen, I married my amazing husband, Tom. Our plan from the beginning was for him to work and earn our living, and for me to stay home and raise our children; we wanted six. This could seem like a large family to many, but to us it was not because Tom had eight siblings, and you will hear about my siblings later. Eight years, five pregnancies, and three living daughters later, we accepted that life had changed our plan.

The loss of a child—whether through miscarriage, stillbirth, Sudden Infant Death, or any other cause of death at an incredibly young age—is a loss like no other. When I lost the two babies due to unexplained miscarriages, I blamed myself. After all they were growing in my body. I thought, *What did I do to cause my body to miscarry them?* So much went through my scattered mind, and I vividly remember thinking I could not give my husband the son he wanted so badly. With both miscarriages I needed a dilation and curettage procedure, a traumatic surgical removal of my baby from my body. The pain of this procedure ripped away our hopes and dreams and pierced our hearts. I remember crying uncontrollably and telling my husband that I was so sorry that my body just could not carry boys. We decided then that, after two miscarriages and the stress of our youngest daughter's repairable birth defect, we could not go through the devastating heartache again.

Those grieving the loss of a child are a special kind of community, though not a group in which anyone seeks or enjoys membership. We all feel alone and isolated, finding we cannot talk about our losses without our friends and family looking for a quick exit or changing the topic of conversation. Women and couples then suffer in silence. Today, counting those of my three daughters, our family has endured nine miscarriages. Sadly, this "special" community of grieving parents is always growing.

I grew up in a large family, the middle of thirteen children. Yep... when I say middle, I mean smack dab in the middle, with four older sisters, four younger sisters, two older brothers and two younger brothers. As if that is not enough middle, I was born in the exact middle of our eighteen-year span in ages.

Have you ever heard of middle-child syndrome? Popular culture defines middle children as forgotten, overlooked, rebellious, or unable to measure up to older or younger siblings. The middle child grows up being either the wild child or a people pleaser who wants everyone to get along. As you read on, I ask you to remember: wild child or people pleaser.

That family experience started me off as a self-development and mindset junkie…and my siblings' frequent advice was rich with opportunity for practicing. In a family with so many voices, I chose to be a listener, and my listening skills are among those I treasure most. Other life tools learned in those growing years also still serve me well: extreme patience, compassion, and empathy.

When life changed our plan for a larger family, I began to dream new dreams for my girls. Two years after my last miscarriage, I was given the opportunity to work outside the home and took a temporary job that later became a permanent position. My work career in the medical field saw coworkers opening up to me. Being that listening ear offered a safe space to talk about their experiences of child loss and other life challenges, where they were truly heard and fully understood.

Decades later, the broader value of all those family-learned skills became evident, as I embarked on an intense self-development and mindset-revision journey at the age of sixty. I discovered that there was so much I still held inside. Yes, a people pleaser and a great listener with compassion and empathy…yet wrapped up in isolation, blame, shame, and low self-worth. And I desperately needed my self-worth to rise! I had allowed low self-esteem to hold me back from too much, including a college education. For my own sake and for the benefit of my growing family—now that grandchildren were being born—I needed to value myself more.

As my July 2019 birthday approached, when I would complete my fifty-ninth year of life, I felt an intense desire to discover who I am and what I want to do in my "senior" years. I set a goal to achieve sixty adventures before the age of sixty . . . and posted that target on social media. I defined *adventure* as anything I had *never* done before.

I began creating my adventure list: thrift shopping *all* day, a hot-air balloon ride, eating at new restaurants, writing a book, skydiving, swimming with sharks, and a cruise to Alaska were a great start! There are fifty-two weeks in a year, and I was going to do sixty adventures—a lofty goal—but I was up for the challenge.

My adventures were rolling along really well until March 2020, and you know what happened then. Pandemic. Quarantines. Shutdowns of public gathering places. "Oh no!" was not my answer. I am not a quitter. I grew up with parents who taught me great work ethics, especially this one: if you start it, you finish it. And I had plenty of time to add to my list . . . July was months away!

I hadn't realized adventures could also be staying locked down in my house, shopping while wearing a mask, attending church online, or having Friday Happy Hour outside in our neighborhood cul-de-sac. So, yes, adventures as I defined them continued! The Alaskan Cruise came off the list, and other adventures were added: hiking every trail within an hour's drive, and starting a podcast.

Probably as for many others, 2020 was the year I discovered my purpose for this season of my life. Between my pandemic-style adventures, there was plenty of time to think about life priorities, to reflect on the past and look differently at the future. All of that adventuring and reflecting carried me full circle to discover my true passion. I now know I am meant to support and serve women who have experienced child loss.

From the first thought of writing a book for those struggling with infertility or the loss of a child during pregnancy or infancy, other ideas followed, such as writing the story of "how I became a grandma the nontraditional way." My three beautiful grandchildren were, respectively, born through a surrogate, with the help of fertility drugs, and with a sperm donor.

Neither of these books is written…yet. My podcast, *Labor Pains*, was my first outlet. This adventure was among the last few of my sixty; I released the first recording in June 2020. Making "adventurous use" of the forced time at home empowered me to learn how to produce and record a podcast at age fifty-nine!

After a couple of months of weekly episodes, I realized more fully the lack of support and resources for this community of women. Searching the internet for online training I could complete quickly to raise my knowledge and competence right away, I found and completed several online grief coaching certification courses, followed by an intense course in Neuro-Linguistic Programming.

As I continued to study how grief affects every person differently, I dug deeply into learning how we each store our experiences uniquely, and realized I was carrying some unresolved grief from an early age, when my mom had a stillborn son. We never talked about Charles; my parents grieved the loss of their fourteenth child alone. A few years ago, I asked my mom about a memory I had of his funeral, that my mom was not there. She confirmed that she had not attended, being still in the hospital. "That was just how they did it back then," she said. My heart broke, now understanding more fully the importance of such closure to the grieving process.

As my studies continued, I discovered other experiences that had prepared me for this new career. The most profound surprise from the past hit me over the head as a "Duh!" I had worked at a funeral home for more than fifteen years and grown up in a grieving home! Life has guided me to help women through one of the most challenging times of their life.

Does my story invite you to open your mind, look back through your life, and seek the multitudes of threads woven through your life to make the tapestry you are today? Are you drawn to sit and allow your subconscious to remind you of the past? Will you allow it to guide you in discovering a glorious purpose for your future?

My process required that forced time of isolation, and I am so grateful for what 2020 gave me. There is joy waiting for you, too, when you can feel and see the path of your life clearly, when you know you are in the right place, doing the right thing. Whatever pain or loss you must face and overcome in life, there can be purpose on the other side.

Teresa Reiniger | Finding Purpose at Sixty

First, Teresa Reiniger is wife to her husband, Tom, since 1979. Proud mother to three beautiful daughters and a kick-ass grandma to three strong-willed grandchildren who will make a mark in this world. After more than fifteen years in the funeral home industry, she is the founding CEO of Living After Grief. A mindset and grief transformation coach and podcast host for *Resilient Moms: Hope, Healing & Living After Loss* (originally called *Labor Pains),* Teresa holds several certifications for grief coaching and is a certified master practitioner and trainer of Neuro-Linguistic Programming and Integrated Time-line Therapy. As she supports women grieving child loss, Teresa's lived experience, wisdom, and training enable her to understand her clients' trauma and loss. Those who are grieving want to feel heard, understood, and to have a compassionate companion to guide them to living again with the love they feel amidst their grief, and Teresa is that person for them.

Dr. Alanna McNelly

Now I Know

Who am I? That's a question some of you may have asked yourselves at least once or, if you're like me, several times a day for the last forty years. I am coming closer to an answer and am now sharing my journey thus far.

I am Dr. Alanna McNelly and Arti's mama. My wife, Sarah, and I have been together for seventeen years. Our beautiful daughter is six years old. I have been around for forty-nine years, and sometimes life can overwhelm me quite a bit. I spent most of my life taking care of others. A bartender for twenty years provided a wide experience of the human condition. Now I manage and treat patients in a high-volume chiropractic office.

I care for others by honoring their wholeness, both dark and light. Knowing we all have an important part to play here on Earth school, I teach people they are worthy and loved as they work through their trauma.

At first tempted to tell my coming-out story, I soon realized it isn't the most important part of my answer to "Who Am I?" Although it was still tough coming out in the late 80s and early 90s, I managed to overcome the homophobia, knowing my worth. My mother and great-grandmother did a fantastic job expressing love and letting me know I was important.

In fact, over the years, many beyond my family helped me discover the answer to "Who Am I?" As I worked my way "out of the closet," my mom's best friend, Pam, was the first person I told. She assured me that I am perfect as I am, and I will always be grateful for that support. She gave me confidence.

There are many damaging illusions society offers about conforming, and being gay is not the only taboo. Being *different* in any way can confuse a life. Seeking acceptance and love as I carried shame for everything odd about me, it turned out that being gay didn't produce the most shame.

Something else inside me felt *weird* even before I knew about sex or intimacy. That bigger shame was because I could see and feel things others could not. Now I know I am an empath.

When I talked with people, or especially if I touched them, I *knew* why they were sad before they told me, even when I was very young. In the church of my childhood, that ability turned into blasphemy because a child couldn't know more than their parents or the pastor. I am not saying I *wasn't* connected to a higher power or that my parents were tyrannical religious fanatics, but the stories I learned early at church and school did not fit the way I was feeling inside.

I spent my early twenties nursing my shame with very poor coping skills. Excessive drinking, relationships that were secret or, at a minimum, emotionally abusive created a serious bout of depression and anxiety that left me empty and suicidal. With a partner who was equally damaged by shame and depression, we became blissfully codependent. Although I became more comfortable with my attraction to women, the depression and anxiety fueled with alcohol met a joint climax that resulted in a two-week stay in treatment center to avoid a suicide attempt.

For this first experience with therapy, I was lucky that the psychiatrist was very good and let me know there was nothing wrong with me. For the first time, someone acknowledged all of me. No longer suicidal but not yet quite understanding my worth, I still thought my value came from what others thought of me.

Then came my first experience of awakening, while waiting tables. A Native American woman, as indicated by her ceremonial clothing, asked to sit in my section. Holding a bag of rocks in her hand, she was not a typical guest at Houlihan's in St. Louis.

As soon as she was seated, she asked if I was aware of my path as a healer. Appearing to listen to someone I couldn't see, she snickered and said, "Your ancestors and guides know you have a job to do." Having just enrolled in massage school, I thought, "Wow! I am twenty-five years old and I finally found my path."

Oh, if only it was that easy.

This unknown visitor told me I had a long path ahead of me, and, thus far, she hasn't been wrong. I spent the next several years trying to be likable, as a good bartender and a great karaoke singer, which satisfied my ego for that time.

Then I met my wife in my early thirties and felt as if she had picked me. Even then she expressed this energy that made you want to be in her light, and she still shines. Meeting her made me want to be better, so I started working on my health and seeing a chiropractor who saved me from being sick all the time. He worked with me on healthier nutrition and alcohol consumption.

He was my inspiration to become a doctor. Again, I thought I had discovered my true path (you get the theme here?). Now a practicing chiropractor, I am also very fortunate to have become a mom in this last decade. My daughter has the same light as my wife, who carried our daughter into this world. I know she picked us to be her parents and is proud of who we are, and who she is, even at six years of age.

These years as Arti's mom stirred something in me again, struggling with that question, "Who Am I?" Striving to be better and help more, I discovered a theme that the harder I work and the more I accomplish, the more I feel a sense of something missing or defeated. I was a doctor, wife, and mom, but what else was I?

Fast-forward to this last winter, when I had another experience of a perfect stranger approaching me and asking, "Are you in the healing arts?" I told him I was, and he casually replied, "You are a part of the Nom." I am still unclear about exactly what he meant, but in that moment his words struck the depths of my soul. The next day, my sister called and asked me if I had ever heard of the Nom.

I asked, astonished, "What did you just say to me?" She explained she heard about it in a podcast and wanted to discuss. My siblings and I have many moments like this when we click with the universe at the same time. The day before, Bill (the stranger) had explained that the Nom are some kind of star people or ancient lineage.

Since then, I have opened my mind to new ideas about how we all fit together. My "anxiety" is no longer a fear, but positive energy in my chest I now identify as power or excitement rather than a negative feeling I need to numb. Alcohol always put my empathic skills to sleep when they were too much for me to tolerate. Now I am developing better coping skills for those times of feeling overwhelmed.

Since the beginning of 2023 I have felt new questions rising in me. What are my gifts? How do I use them? Why can't I figure this out? I am also aware that many of us are feeling this same surge in feelings. I know they are real, friends, and here for a reason. I had an epiphany in this summer of 2023, through yet another experience of someone trying to beat my worth into my head.

My friend Cara, who identifies as Dragon Mother, invited me to a Temescal sweat lodge, a ceremony that forces you to see yourself. This sacred event let me see my worth. All my shame, all my insecurities and my gifts are one . . . and she is Earth Mother. I am all that is!

Heads up! So are you. We are always looking for the *thing out there* that can answer that eternal question, "Who Am I?" And the answer is inside us. We each have the ability to have it all.

I am—we are—not only connected to God, Spirit, or Source but are the actual embodiment of that higher spirit. We are here to experience life on Earth—every bit of life: the good, the bad, the ugly, and the amazing, all at once.

After all this time telling everyone how much I love them, I didn't know how to love myself. But this summer as I wrote this chapter, I learned that loving myself first and then loving others is the key to rising into my greatness.

I no longer walk in fear because now I *know* my true purpose at last: I *am* sacred ground. I am important, as are you, and we are all in this together.

Dr. Alanna McNelly | Now I Know

Dr. Alanna McNelly began her journey in Grafton, Illinois, in the mystical Mississippi river valley near St. Louis, Missouri, and one of the most beautiful spots in the Midwest. Raised by wonderful parents as the oldest of four children, Alanna currently lives in a suburb of St. Louis with her amazing wife, Sarah, and their beautiful daughter, Artis. Many jobs—teacher, bartender, realtor, and massage therapist—prepared her for her path to her work today as a chiropractic physician. Alanna practices acupuncture, massage, reiki, and other healing modalities seeking to help people with their trauma, both physical and emotional. She aspires to accept all that humanity presents and aid in the healing each of us needs. Alanna welcomes both the yin and yang, the light and dark, the male and the female, and all the diverse energy that results from living on this Earth school.

Ann Bender

Living Thru Death's Eyes

She and a few other residents followed the barely visible outline of the staff counselor down a dimly lit corridor to a massive iron door. The air smelled stagnant and felt thick as she breathed. Fear filled her at the sobbing cringe from the rusted hinges, as the staff struggled against the overwhelming weight of the entrance. She tried to adjust her eyes to the desperate blackness of the tunnel. Yet she could see nothing and felt only a suffocating heaviness like a boulder on a blanket under which she was sleeping.

Why did she want so badly to join this guided tour into the forbidden ancient hospital building across the street? She heard another staff counselor inform the tiny group that the light switch was at the other end of the tunnel. Now, her heart racing in her throat and pounding in her ears, she followed on.

She forced her legs to move her along the tunnel, thick with darkness. As she stepped, the crunch beneath her feet sent jarring goosebumps through her. What was the source of each hollow crunch? And what the hell was she thinking going into this darkness?

In the weeks leading up to this staff-guided tunnel trip, she had repeatedly *seen* a patient through the windows of the supposedly abandoned psychiatric asylum across the driveway from her own place of confinement. Before this moment, she'd only seen glimpses of his filthy hospital gown that failed to cover his hairy buttocks. Because the windows in the old asylum were thick with layers of dirt and debris, she never had a clear *view* with her special form of sight. On one occasion, he turned, and his dark, bloodshot eyes stared boldly from between his lanky red hair and unkempt beard. She wanted to understand why he was in that building. In fact, she wanted to understand everything about him as a ghost. Why couldn't *everyone* see, hear, feel, smell, and interact with the spirit world?

The staff counselors kept telling her it was her imagination. Other patients, truly disturbed ones, also saw things through those windows, but she knew she was not suffering their hallucinations. She was desperate for answers, just beginning to realize her special ability, shared by few others. But back then she could not have known what or who was coming.

In the months leading up to her psychiatric hospitalization at the tender age of fifteen, she was filled with overwhelming isolation and depression. Since earliest childhood, an outcast because of her ability to see dead people, she was just beginning to gain the new skill of separating her own emotions from those of these beings beyond the veil. For more than a dozen years she'd been tormented by vivid dreams of unknown events—some still in the future and some prior to her birth. Even family members she trusted didn't understand how she could know the unknown or, at least for her, the unknowable. She found no safe place to shelter from the unseen world of ghosts. The spiral downward was a short one, from early lack of family support to desperate cries for help in the form of suicide attempts.

Years later, in an adult revisioning, I blinked and felt myself back in the suffocating blackness of the tunnel from my teens. Seemingly back in my fifteen-year-old body, I moved again into the black abyss, my heart racing. As a slight glimmer of light appeared before me, a wave of relief was quickly replaced by fear. I knew I needed to face the terrifying man in the abandoned hospital at the end of that tunnel; I had to face what haunted my nightmares. I knew he was not simply a scary man who few of us could see; the *unseen* is multi-layered.

The white light from the end of the tunnel blinded me. This time, I froze in place until the staff counselor jolted me to continue walking. Focusing on the stairs I had to traverse, I felt I was being watched. A gut-wrenching swarm of feelings swept over me, covering the spectrum of all emotions. Now more mature in self-awareness, I could finally realize that all along my feelings of dire desperation might not have been my own. A full fifteen years after that teenage experience, I had begun to understand that I did not just "see" ghosts but emotionally interacted with them.

As the revisioning continued, I found myself at the top of the steps up out of the tunnel. The doorway to a huge, open room was on my right. I slowly peeked inside and saw the same disheveled man in the hospital gown. I blinked and he locked eyes with me. I blinked again and he was instantly ten feet closer. I again closed my eyes, praying this was not real, just as I had at fifteen. I opened them, and he was in my face!

In that instant of pure terror, I realized that I mirrored what he *felt*. His anger at being incarcerated for his love of drink. His fury from being tortured by electrocution to curtail his emotions. And his deep sadness for a life fullfilled lost. In my moment of paralyzing fear, feeling his anger and pain, I knew I had to help him. He did not know he was dead. So with my thoughts, I told him he was no longer living.

What happened next is nearly impossible to put into words. I visualized a blinding white light, like the one seen earlier on this revisit as the end of the tunnel drew near. In my mind, I showed him the next part of his journey. I guided his crossing from our world to the next. Even at this point in life, I had no road map or guidance for what I was doing. I simply followed what my heart told me.

In that moment of facing my greatest darkness, I found my path. He literally scared me into an understanding of my unique abilities. I looked around the room—which had just been empty in my second-sight vision—and now "saw" how it once looked, filled with patients and archaic equipment. Everything looked shadowy, gray, and not solid, confirming I was glimpsing the past. I blinked again and the shadows were gone. With the intention "show me more" in my mind, I blinked slowly once more, and the ancient objects reappeared, more detailed.

I could have stood there all day, but I felt called to continue through the ancient building. The remainder of the walk was filled with dust and cobwebs. The intense feeling of being watched never eased up. In my soul, I understood I was being watched. And I knew that few people were able to help the lost spirits of the past.

It's taken years to fine-tune my skills for helping these beings who others don't see, while maintaining my sanity. Living with the sight of the dearly departed has been my silent struggle for years. This battle reached its climax when I lived in Spokane, Washington, at twenty-four years old.

I began dreaming through the eyes of a woman who was being chased through dry, grassy fields, pursued by an attacker. She was breathless, naked, and about to be brutally killed. I would wake covered in sweat and shaking in fear. By now, I knew from experience that this was not *my* dream. The details were so vivid that I knew the precise location of the attack. I also knew this woman was no longer alive.

A few months passed, and a very similar dream happened again. My perspective in the *sight* was as the same attacker, but a different woman and different field, one less than a mile from my home. Similar dreams continued every few months, and in two months I could clearly identify the location of the brutal rapes and murders.

To better understand what I was "receiving," I drove to the locations I could identify. For two different women, I *saw* the woman's body. In each case, the bodies were at the edge of a wooded area beyond a dried field. The attacks were vicious, continuing even after the murderer suffocated her. I did not have the courage to go to either body and wanted to inform the authorities. I still did not put together what I was *seeing* in my mind's eye with the local serial murders of sex workers.

About a year later, I watched my neighbor drive home in his van, finding it odd when moments later he drove past again in a white sports car. Planting a magnolia tree in my yard, I locked eyes with him on his third drive-by. My heart sank, as his once-blue eyes appeared jet black. All my nightmares made sense in that instant, but it was months (and many more nightmares) later that my neighbor was arrested for those murders of multiple women.

One of the women he murdered had been buried under his bedroom window the very day we locked eyes. I decided to move out of state following all the drama and to never again withhold information that might bring a criminal to justice. My amazing husband set one rule that I gladly honor: No cases close to home!

Today, I spend my life actively helping both spirits and the living. I learned that it is not enough to occasionally lend aid; I must help every day. I find my peace and balance in life by honoring rather than ignoring my abilities, which had caused me far more suffering. In fact, because of my sixth sense, I now run toward my fears. And because our daughter shares my gifts, she will always have a safe place of understanding and support. I learned the hard way that no child should have to face interactions with dead people alone.

Ann Bender | Living Thru Death's Eyes

Ann Bender's journey in life includes seeing the long-departed, starting in very early childhood. When she shared her experience, her family reacted with fear. It would be decades before Ann learned that some "memories" were of events prior to her birth, involving people she'd never met while they lived. Some of the stories she *saw* were secrets buried by her family for good reasons. Today, Ann no longer suffers in silence, sharing her gifts with many across diverse religious and spiritual beliefs. She also receives nonverbal messages from animals to communicate what they want and need. When she is not channeling or writing, Ann creates gemstone works of wearable art, is a master dowser, and an educator on the paranormal. Helping the living thrive longer, Ann also works as a health coach. Her hope for future generations born with the gift of "sight" is that they know they are not alone.

Danielle Solito

Look Up

When I was a young girl, God gave me a desire to be a mom, along with the hope of staying home to raise my children. At the age of twenty, pregnant with my first child but attending college and working full time, I felt that hope fading. I dreamt of raising a family in a small town, close to the country, where neighborhood friends could ride their bikes and play with friends in the streets. I wanted my children to have a life similar to mine as a 1980s kid, with carefree summers and a sense of belonging. Living in the Bay Area on a tight budget made that dream seem no longer an option.

When my daughter was three, I met a man who would become my husband five years later. At the time we met, life was a little crazy. In fact, I was in a custody battle for my daughter from a previous relationship and was working simultaneously to heal from residual family trauma.

I have learned that there are moments in life that separate a *before* from a tragically different *after*. Such moments change the course of life. They redefine a person. My defining moment was waking up to sixty missed calls on the morning of November 19, 2009.

The previous night, my twin brothers had been over for dinner—their favorite meal, a recipe from our great-grandmother. As far as I knew, they had returned home safely and all was well. But sadly, Jonathan didn't wake up the next morning. He was my best friend, whom I loved and defended fiercely. At the age of twenty, with no reasonable explanation, he was gone.

Two weeks after Jonathan passed away, my boyfriend Jason lost his job. Life was a blur. It felt as if we could get no relief. This was our test. We were overcome with sorrow and yet we pushed through, continuing looking to God for direction and confirmation that we were on the right path.

Eventually the autopsy records revealed the cause of Jonathan's death as accidental asphyxiation, the consequence of a misdiagnosed heart condition. A year after Jonathan passed, we found that his twin, Jordan, had the same condition and would need a permanent pacemaker implanted.

But we weren't done yet! Also a year after Jonathan's death, I was diagnosed with a myocardial bridge. Although it's a common condition, surgery is needed in severe cases. My condition called for invasive surgery, removing a part of my heart muscle to free the artery that was being compressed with each heartbeat.

At the age of twenty-seven I had invasive heart surgery, which would require after-care support from friends and family. After two months, I went back to work and found myself rapidly excelling in my position. I felt I had stepped into my purpose and our family was now on the right track.

Then, just three more months later, my heart condition worsened. The surgeon let me know that, though the surgery worked to free one artery affected by the myocardial bridge, we discovered there was another myocardial bridge that couldn't be freed. I was told I may never be able to have another child.

Jason and I had talked of having children, and now I found myself too disabled to work full time. I felt stuck. I felt lost, as our world once again turned upside down.

Reaching for familiar support, we began attending church more regularly, praying for God's direction. We prayed for strength to get through the months ahead, prayed for our little family, and for the blessings we knew God had for us. At the time, we couldn't yet see those blessings, but we waited in faith, staying true to God's Word. It was a time of trials requiring complete trust that God would provide for our family.

We were married four years later, and with the help of my amazing cardiology team at Stanford and the obstetrics unit at Lucile Packard Children's Hospital, we welcomed our daughter, Emma. She was just as perfect as my first daughter. It was at that moment I knew the prayers I had prayed in childhood were being answered, one by one. The silver lining to my heart condition was that I would be a stay-at-home mom!

The dream I'd had of being home with my older daughter, Ava—volunteering at school, participating in field trips, and other fun activities—had come to fruition. When Emma was born, I got to relish each baby moment with her, and she quickly became the class mascot at Ava's school.

Of course, our life was full of ups and downs, as all lives are: we moved and lived through job changes and evolving family issues. However, we continued to look up to God, praying to the one we knew would lead us where we needed to go. Three years after the birth of Emma, with the help of my amazing medical teams, we welcomed our son, Mason. I could now embark upon the blissful craziness of being an at-home mom to three kids.

I didn't tell Jason, but I continued to pray that God would move us to one of the favorite places I had lived as a child. It was important to me to raise my kids in a safe community, where they could play outside until the streetlights came on and ride their bikes to their friends' houses. As a child, I had moved fourteen times by the time I turned twelve, and

I wanted something more stable and consistent for my children. While it seemed out of reach, I never stopped praying for it. We had launched a five-year plan to get out of the deteriorating city we lived in, without knowing where we would end up.

In April 2020 God answered our prayers and we moved to my favorite childhood town. God did it for us! Then, He pushed me further and began showing what His purpose was for me in this season.

Through the years of raising a family, I found that a mom can lose herself, not just mentally, but physically. I love being a mom and yet I realized my personal health had been on the back burner during pregnancy and nursing. My lack of energy and inability to keep up with my growing children made that obvious. I began praying for a change, for the power to be consistent in making changes while the entire world was freaking out about a pandemic. I reached out to a long-time friend who looked stunning after losing more than a hundred pounds. I wanted what she had. The energy, the glow, the clarity, the confidence that exuded from her. She stepped up and coached me to lose more than sixty pounds!

This change alone helped grow my confidence, and then my cardiologist saw a substantial and positive change in my lipid panels and was very optimistic for the future. After losing weight, I was more comfortable stepping into the role God had for me. I paid my gift forward to many of my friends and family, starting my own service of health coaching, which allowed me to bring in extra income to cover those little stresses that stretch a family from time to time. I knew God was asking me to encourage others and show them it's possible to do hard things with the right mindset. God had my full attention.

As I increasingly look up, listening to divine guidance, I develop myself in new ways. I know God has me here as a mom and safe haven for my children. With confidence I stand up and fight for my children in whatever way possible. With that expanding help from God, and in His strength, I'm able to empower other parents to speak up and fight for their children's rights. He has provided me with the opportunity to lead a group of parents in the fight for their children, showering them with words of encouragement and with confidence to make a change in their children's lives. He has given me back my freedom and power.

God knew what He was doing when our family was hit with the devastating loss of my brother and I became permanently disabled. He was preparing me for the answers to my prayers, but only if I was faithful during the hard times of waiting. The surprising silver lining of my heart condition blessed me with the opportunity to be the best mom and wife I can be, living in the small hometown I loved so much as a little girl.

Sometimes life has to fall apart so God can put it back together as He had planned. Now, whenever those tough times appear, I remember to look up.

Danielle Solito | Look Up

Danielle Solito is a wife, mom to three kids, a heart patient, and health coach. Living in the Bay Area in California for the last twenty years, she attended college to pursue a business degree, then become a full-time, stay-at-home mom. Danielle spends her days doting on her family, playing with her German Shepherd, and tending to her health clients. In her free time, she is an advocate for her children and inspires other parents to speak up for their parental rights. She loves to explore new areas, hike the beautiful trails near her home, and spend time at the beach—especially in Carmel-by-the-Sea, where she and her husband often escape.

Sequoia Haskell

All Masters Were Once Disasters

After healing my burns overnight in hospital, rather than having rats' skin as a graft, I embarked on a four-year spiritual development course. There, I fine-tuned my clairvoyance and healing abilities, cleared past lives, soothed my inner child, and so much more. Through this experience, I realized that, unless we do deep inner work, our spiritual gifts are of no use.

The first part of my life, inflicted with trials and tribulations that so many of us can relate to, led me on a quest. And I left no stone unturned on the path of self-discovery and healing. I was broken inside, had no self-worth, and stumbled through life, making so many poor choices. Yet, at my core, I knew there was a reason for it all. No matter what I went through, I knew I would be OK, and that an angel always accompanied me, especially when I felt that all hope was lost.

As a wounded healer, I began my journey thirty-eight years ago in New Zealand. It was a time of powerful awakening. Incredible books seemed to fall into my lap encouraging me to follow the calling of my soul, to find the truth with a group of single mums; we created a community of support and strength in the raising of children. This potent and powerful sisterhood paved the way from there to here as we discovered ourselves and our gifts, with an insatiable appetite for growth and expansion.

Moving to Australia with two of my four children led me on this new path. We then moved thirty times in five years, were homeless four times, and went hungry many times during that period. Despite surviving all that plus three floods, two bush fires, and daily life in the heart of the bush without power or a vehicle, we always managed to find a solution. We not only thrived but survived! This five-year passage in our lives taught us resilience, strength, resourcefulness, and total trust and faith in a higher power. Every experience gave me deeper empathy for and understanding of the plights of others.

Homelessness, for example. There is no scarier feeling than having nowhere to go, no address to call home. Nowhere to shower, or even to sleep. All of that is much harder with two children in tow. We lived in a tourist town. We would move into a place, then be told it had been sold and that we had to move out. But there was always a miracle or an angel to save the day. The experience taught us to take nothing for granted. I met some of the most incredible people, each with their own unique story to tell.

During those five years, I channelled a vision for humanity. The more challenges and miracles my family experienced, the more I could see what people really needed. Food, shelter, warmth, a comfortable bed, and a shower. Basic human needs that we all take for granted come first, and then people need community, support, and a sense of belonging.

The vision itself is amazing: self-sufficient communities in which each member shares their gifts and all members' needs are met. I saw schools that taught self-awareness, communication, and the life skills to thrive. Everyone was financially abundant and living joyful lives.

That vision is now ready to come to fruition. The journey to this point brought growth and evolution and has shown *all* things are possible. As I healed more of my own false beliefs, I shared that knowledge with others, building a client base all around the world. I have clearly seen that there is nothing that self-love and compassion cannot overcome.

The deeper empathy I now feel as a result of my experiences makes me an exceptional healer. Yes, exceptional! We all need to own our magnificent brilliance, and I took a long time to do that, as I am now fifty-eight. I began questioning: when is healing enough? When is my best good enough? And the answer has come: Now!

I am whole and healed. I am perfectly imperfect. I love who I am! I am outright amazing! There is no obstacle I cannot overcome. Nothing needs fixing in me because I am not broken. I have value and worth, and what others think of me is none of my business. I do not need anyone to validate me; what you see is what you get. If you do not like it, leave! This is a journey of overcoming, and forever becoming, for each and every one of us.

We are rapidly moving into the most magical time of awakening and ascension in the history of humanity. We each chose to come here, at this time, to stand in our full magnificence, power, and beauty. We have come through lifetimes of persecution on every level.

We are all still here, more powerful than ever before. They will torture and persecute us *no* more. Together we stand, the Divine Goddess risen. We are no longer slaves to the internal prison! Allow me to guide you to give yourself back to You, with this poem as my gift.

Dark to Light

Nothing in this world is real. The meaning of everything is the meaning I give it.
Where does one begin to tell the story of the heroine's journey?
How does one condense a multifaceted and complex being into merely one chapter?
So many lifetimes, dimensions of time and space, have been crammed into this one incarnation.

Do I begin with the tumultuous childhood, fraught with abuse,
    neglect, and an individual with a predatory nature, who
    underpins the victim's shame and self-blame, which permeated
    every fibre of my being.
Every cell, every vein.
Or is it better to cite the teens, the coming of age,
Finding all the doorways to channel the rage.
"I'll do what I want! I have no fear!
Does anyone care, let alone hear?"
The world is so perilous to navigate alone.
No one to guide you,
Nobody's home!
Maybe it's the twenties, when it really begins.
No cares in the world, no responsibilities, only invincibility.
"Looking for love in all the wrong places,"
Dangerous choices, in faraway spaces!
And then…it's love. "Oh it's so meant to be."
"I will love you forever, to eternity."
And then tears and heartbreak follow,
Trauma so deep for a heart that is broken,
Until…
Out of the corner of the eye,
The next guy, you allow to use and abuse you.
But still you try and try!
Finally, bliss!
Parenting happens and, oh, what a shock!
Nothing prepares for the oceans of tears and passing on of hereditary
    fears.
The marital bed, far from serene,
offered worse hardships to shame and demean.
Violence, rape, rejection, abuse,
maintaining the illusion of being of no use.
From my deepest wounds

come my greatest gifts.
They arm me with weapons and tools, to fight for my bliss.
They make each one a mirror, to look deep inside,
To peel back the layers,
To no longer hide.
The pain endured has brought me here,
To choose between darkness or light, to live without fear.
Choosing to grow or not?
Never happy, no flow.
The coal or the diamond,
They both are the same.
This is: you, this is me, whatever the name.
To learn the lesson to trust was hard. I am still on my way,
Healing myself and others each day.
Nights spent in grief for times gone by
now being replaced with a truth that can last.
Loving one's self means losing the mask.
A phoenix rises from the hungriest of flames.
I healed my own wounds, and my "Real" eyes remain. With hope as
    my armour, my whole body went up in flames.
Knowing with my new name arising.
The nurses perplexed, seeing my burns gone.
The power of visioning, I had all along.
Self-Love is a truth.
No longer a song.
Heart fully opened to receive Divine Light.
I can now overcome any plight.
This is the way to the truth that I know,
Which was imbued within me so long ago.
Finding truth in my heart, for this is my glow.
We each write the chapters of our own books.
It is beautiful inside, journeying deep within.
There is really nowhere else to look.

Sequoia Haskell | All Masters Were Once Disasters

Every encounter and hardship is an opportunity
To blossom and glow,
To swim with the current and allow life to flow.
Only then will you awaken to welcome the dawn,
And remember your divinity, from where you were born.
A wounded healer is a force to behold.
I have discovered there is gold, hammered no more,
I have broken the mold.
Life's twists and turns were roughly trod,
They forged a being that is now perfectly shod.
I am part of a plan to clear and ascend,
To falter and fail, to find ways to amend.
This is the task I came here for, no "mistakes," but lessons on how to
    endure.
Always a blessing,
Always a cure.
This vessel, this form, imperfectly acts
to discover what is real,
To discern and sort lies from facts.
The babes that I birthed give me deep and sublime love,
Opened my heart with a joy that is divine.
If we look for ourselves
In their innocent eyes, we will see
That truth wears no disguise.
Do not seek others to tell you your worth,
As you chose to come and shine Light on this Earth.
I love you; I love you,
To thine own self be true.
In the word Imperfect, is I'm perfect,
This is me; this is you.
You are me; I am you.
I am whole. I am healed, and so, too, are you.
Hi. I am Sequoia. I began my journey as Anne.

Sequoia Haskell is an international clairvoyant/healer, sharing her gifts for almost forty years. She has mastered many modalities, including tapping, reiki, the compassion key, and hypnosis, combining their essentials into her own process, which she calls Sh*t-Shifting. Sequoia is here to raise the vibration and consciousness of humanity, and to bring light to the planet in this time of awakening. She works with groups and individuals, assisting thousands of clients to heal their inner child, resolve past lives, and clear deep trauma. She is a well-known clairvoyant in her home country of New Zealand and in Australia, where she now lives. Sequoia discovered her power as a healer when, after being badly burnt, one of the burns wouldn't heal. Successfully *willing* her burn to heal launched her on a lifetime journey to learn and share modalities of self-healing.

Nicole Tucker

Shattering the Mask

Trauma.

Childhood trauma.

Childhood sexual trauma.

Any of these words can catapult a person into an abyss of pain and suffering. If you know, you know. If you don't know, then embrace that ignorance with gratitude and be glad you don't know. I certainly didn't understand its impact on my future self when it happened to me.

I was twelve, and I already suffered from insomnia. I couldn't sleep because I knew he would come into my room. Not a monster in an imaginary way but a monster nonetheless: an uncle who lived with us. I couldn't lie there, simply waiting. That young, I started sneaking out, drinking, and smoking cigarettes with my best friend. I wanted to ease the pain of what was happening and the pain of growing up too fast.

Then, one night, I got caught sneaking back inside. Climbing through the window, I found myself looking at my father, sitting on my bed. I was in trouble. He yelled, I yelled. He yelled some more. Then, finally, I broke down and told him why I was sneaking out, and about my uncle's abuse.

He didn't believe me. I was just a sneaky, lying, preteen brat. My dad kicked my uncle out, but soon he started coming around again, and

I never spoke of the past. I had to accept that my family didn't see the sexual abuse as an issue for them, and they still thought I was lying.

Life continued with no consequences for his actions, and I had to see him at family events. I learned to cope and act as if I wasn't hurting. Silenced by disbelief, I avoided thinking about the abuse at all costs. So I "moved on."

The silence inside me was deafening. It was killing my worth one moment at a time while adding anxiety issues related to trust, safety, and security. I was in survival mode for many years. Numb, distant, unworthy, unhealthy…Every day I wore a plastic face. The smile frozen, the eyes touched by tears invisible to everyone but me. As time went on, the mask hardened until I didn't know how to be something different. I was stuck, and it went on for years like that.

Thus, twenty-ish years later, my life was still messy, just on a much larger scale. Having three kids and settling for a loveless, touchless marriage was not ideal or healthy. Trapped and miserable barely described how I felt. Always thinking I did not deserve a loving relationship, I had settled for anyone showing a shred of stability. Did I deserve happiness and an intimate, loving relationship? In my head, no. I was not worthy. I was tainted and disgusting. I still held myself responsible for the actions of another person, who was the adult.

With no family support, and hiding my history from everyone else, I felt utterly alone, unseen by even myself. I was alone in my marriage and alone in the shell of a human being I had become. Guilt and shame settled over my mind and heart like two constricting spiderwebs as I spun an outer web of lies to "prove" my plastic mask's reality. Any feelings that didn't fit that fixed smile were hidden, held in check. Ignoring and burying my own reality also meant I was easy to trigger, and I experienced terrifying panic attacks daily. Living in continuous shame and regret, I was driven to people-pleasing at its best, while staying super-humanly busy. The art of living numb and in hiding isn't so hard once you collect all the right tools.

My healing finally began when, at thirty-nine years of age, I confronted my mom. I saw one too many posts on social media with photos of her hugging my uncle, laughing and enjoying concerts together. They were living it up while I suffered. I lashed out, heartbroken, crying tears of anger and confusion. I screamed at her, asking, "Why would I still be saying this all these years later if it were not true?"

This moment carried significance and impact for us both. All at once, it was like a switch was flipped. She suddenly realized that I was telling the truth. If I was lying, why was I still bringing it up all these years later? She finally saw the suffering I had endured alone. The switch flipped for me when I finally felt heard. I realized that she had never heard me because I hid. If I *did* bring it up, I wasn't loud enough. Nobody heard me.

In that moment, she understood and finally spoke the apology I had needed for so long. That changed everything, knowing my mom supported me. Always my best friend, even when I was hurting, now she knows me better and hears me. We are closer because of it.

Mom also reminded me that I had *one* life to live. I can never return to that time in the past, but I can always change the time that is my future. She made me think, and she was right.

I had already wasted many years in a loveless and touchless marriage. I had found my voice, and I was worthy of being heard! It took twenty-seven years for me to stand up for myself, and when I did I did it in a big way. I left my dead marriage after fifteen years of boredom. I moved my kiddos back to our home state to have a support system nearby. I started seeing a counselor and unpacking old trauma. Who was I now? I did not know. Discovering what I wanted in life took a lot of soul-searching and learning new skills, like trusting myself and others, conquering my fear of people not liking me, and slowing down my unhealthy people-pleasing. Perhaps most importantly, I learned to believe in myself.

Soon, I was content. I started a new and loving relationship. My life was healing and growing, but I was still having triggers. I still had panic attacks out of the blue. Sometimes, I was still spinning out of control and didn't know why.

Then I found a retreat in Utah by the Younique Foundation…a week-long expense-paid retreat for childhood sexual abuse survivors. It was, indeed, unique, and it changed my life. They taught us about our brains—specifically the limbic system—and how we can develop new neural pathways and how old ones can weaken, thanks to the brain's ability to adapt. I learned techniques for coping with and breathing through the triggers. I came home a much better and calmer person. I finally knew I was worthy and made it my mission to tell people about my experience. My time to help others had arrived. I have a full voice again, and I am using it.

Listen. We *all* have a voice! Do not tell yourself you are not worthy. Do not tell yourself you don't deserve happiness, love, abundance, courage, strength, acceptance, belief, and more. We all deserve it. Our trauma and our past *do not* define us. But our ability to sit in that reality and accept it for what it is will be the catalyst to begin living again. Even the tiniest steps move us toward healing and strength.

I know some family members still do not believe me, even today. But convincing them is not my job. Just because I have a voice doesn't mean everyone who hears my story accepts it. Listen to me—I do not have to convince others of the truth, nor do you. Sit with that for a moment. Fill your heart with that thought and let it go. We are more than any crumb of doubt others carry; that is their burden.

Taking care of myself was a highly effective part of the healing process and regaining my power. That power was shredded by the abuse and then stripped away by my family's doubt and my unhealthy coping strategies. I went from being a beautiful and happy twelve-year-old young lady to a shamed and hurting twelve-year-old wounded child. That shame and hurt followed me for thirty-two years until that Younique retreat. All those decades, it never left me; it was inside me every day. I suffered assault at twelve and continued to suffer from the trauma and lack of family support. My dad remained in denial until the day he died. That is a pain I still live with now.

Having found my voice again, I use it now in service. I speak for all the silent victims. I speak out for protecting children. 1 am aware of the signs and symptoms of sexual abuse and notice them in your children. We are meant to be children's protectors and advocates. If they come to you, believe them. If they say they do not like a person, ask them questions. Do not ignore concerns about family members. Statistically, more than 90 percent of abusers are *people children know, love, and trust,* 30 to 40 percent are abused by a family member, and 50 percent by someone whom they know and trust outside the family. Typically, children don't make up accusations of sexual abuse on their own. Show children the love and respect they deserve, and affirm their voice. You empower them to tell their shameful secrets.

We have all had pain and trauma in our lives at some point. My experience is applicable to everyone, not just sexual abuse survivors. My journey relied on perseverance and bravery, once I shattered the plastic mask. I put forth consistent effort to understand my trauma, knowing this was not a bag for someone else to unpack. I took responsibility every day in the fight with my inner self, with distorted thinking, and with negative self-talk. Fighting it down on the daily is still an issue. But I stay brave, facing it every day. I recognize how far I have come and the strength it has required to do so.

Survivor.

Childhood Trauma Survivor.

Childhood Sexual Trauma Survivor. This is me.

Nicole Tucker is a business banking officer with Enterprise Bank and Trust. Also a makeup artist with Seint Official, her passion is to bring confidence to women through makeovers and teaching makeup application. In her spare time, Nicole loves to spend time with her sweetie, kids, grandkids, and two adorable fur babies. Some of her other passions include reading, biking, traveling, camping, and pretty much anything outdoors. In 2022 she started a new job and welcomed other big personal and professional changes, including getting engaged after dating for eight years and becoming a published author. Nicole has lived in St. Louis most of her life except for three years in the beautiful mountains of Steamboat Springs, Colorado.

Jan Kraus

Once Upon a Friendship

Futility, and something close to madness, overwhelmed me. I might have overcome the pain and loss, but then came that final blow. Oh, how I wished I was still unhappy and confused. Instead, I was shattered and desolate.

Once Upon a Time...
Best Friend and I traveled together, regularly chose adventure over comfort, and shared our hopes and dreams. She was always dating some fellow. I was shy with men, so she often tried to fix me up with her current beau's friends, but blind dates were not for me. She and I roomed together for a short time but eventually were happier living apart.

Then...
I fell deeply in love with Prince Charming, an intensely thoughtful, captivating, and somewhat mysterious man. The romance flamed hot for months and was still vital and consuming for me. But then I felt him withdraw, without explanation.

I had not seen Best Friend for a while. She often withdrew when she began a new romance. I didn't worry, as she always sought me out when the novelty wore off. So I was not surprised when she dropped by one evening, unannounced and glowing with complacency.

"How are things with you and Prince Charming?" she asked.

I thought I should share the insecurities I felt. I had sensed him pulling away, and I was confused and sad. Yet some primitive instinct gave me pause.

I said, untruthfully, "He's been busy, but we are good."

Best Friend looked confused. She blurted out, "I don't know how to say this, but Prince Charming and I have been seeing each other. We are in love."

"What?" I asked as the room spun.

Words rushed out of her mouth. All I heard was "Prince Charming and I." "Prince Charming and I." "Prince Charming and I."

She wanted to talk it out. "I had to let you know, didn't I?"

In a high, shrill voice, I said, "Talk it out? Talk it out? What is wrong with you?" I am not a violent person, but I wanted to thrash her somehow, some way.

Later, I could not remember how I got her out the door.

Best Friend and my lover. Best Friend and my lover.

Those words echoed through my brain and embedded themselves in my heart during the seemingly endless days that followed. I went through the motions of life, but misery and pain were constant companions. Bitter bile ran through my body now instead of blood, and acid in place of spittle.

I could not share my grief with anyone else. I was so confused. I loved Prince Charming. I loved Best Friend. I wanted to hate them both, but I did not know how. So I kept the anguish to myself. I gradually realized I would have to live with it.

Six Months Later...

"Join me for a drink?" she called and begged. I tried to refuse. Really, I did. My feelings toward Former Best Friend were so jumbled. But, in spite of my misgivings, I steeled myself and joined her at a little bar near my home.

I found her in a fury. "Prince Charming is an awful man. He wasn't at all serious. How can he be so cruel?" The theme of this one-way conversation was *Join the Hate Prince Charming Club!* She would be president, and I, her minion.

Her face registered both confusion and fascination when I said, "I truly love him. I cannot hate someone I love." What I did not say was, *I cannot even hate you.*

As quickly as I could break away, I left her. I felt that Former Best Friend and I were now utterly estranged.

My depression deepened over the next few months, which still included a couple of painful forays into her world. She took up with a married man and did not understand why I would not double-date with his married friend. She called periodically and shared her angst. I kept answering her calls.

Sometimes, I am a slow learner.

That Final Blow…

Breaking several months of silence, her bright voice was again on the phone. "Come over tonight?"

"Oh, I don't think so. I'm not…"

"Oh, please. You must see my new apartment. I'm having a few people over. I really want you here." She pressed me and—foolishly—I said yes.

She opened the door, once again all aglow. She fluttered around, serving drinks, smiling like a specter with a secret. "I want you to meet someone," she said and presented Princess.

Then she dropped the bomb. "I introduced Princess and Prince Charming a couple of months ago. They've already set the date," she said with a chilling glee. My living nightmare had a new player.

Princess was tall, slender, pretty, sweet, and other-worldly. A minister's daughter, no less! Princess was the ideal match to Prince Charming's persona. Really, that is what hurt the most. Princess was the perfect mate for his deepest vision of what he wanted and could be.

The final pieces of my heart fell bleeding at their feet. But Former Best Friend did not notice.

That Night…

Somehow, I got home.

The betrayal was complete. Best Friend stole my lover, threw him away, then introduced him to the woman he would marry. And worst of all, she purposefully played it all out in front of me as if it was a gift, oblivious to the depth of my despair.

That night was hellacious. Time was unbearable. I could not sit, could not stand, could not lie down. There was no comfort. I paced and ranted through the darkness.

Dawn came as a terrible surprise.

I am spiritual but not religious. Out of pure desperation, I tried to pray. I knelt in the middle of my living room, tears streaming down my face, early daylight filtering through the sheer curtains.

I put my hands together. But before I could utter an entreaty, like a bolt of lightning, a voice filled my being.

You are the only person in this room who can fix this! Get up!

An immense flush of emotion ran through me. I was struck dumb by a revelation and a regeneration. The relief was enormous. I was astounded.

I had been acting the fool. I had allowed this abuse. But no more! No longer a victim, I would rise above the melodrama. Return to sanity. Return to true love. Find and cherish myself.

I would not close off my heart. I would not succumb to extremes of cynicism, hatred, or self-flagellation. I would not lose my vulnerability, although I was now more mindful of risk.

When I got up off my knees, I stood on my pinnacle of personal strength.

Ever After...

Former Best Friend's drama did not end, but I no longer participated emotionally. She embarked on a campaign to find a marriageable partner, dating heavily until Nice Guy asked her. I adroitly played my role in her wedding. But I was an actress in a play that had to be brought to the final curtain.

Nice Guy and Former Best Friend moved out of state to be near his family. The relocation was a gift. We lost touch… apparently by distance; but actually, on my part, by design.

I forgave her, but I could never forget.

Prince Charming and Princess married, and I never saw either of them again. I truly wish them all the happiness they are capable of attaining. Princess was the innocent in this tawdry tale, and I hope she pulls Prince Charming up with her love.

I forgave him, but I could never forget.

I now know my survival depends upon avoiding the snares of abuse, manipulation, and undue self-deprecation. I might not yet have found full understanding, but I found hope.

I found mercy and a higher purpose when I reached beyond the hurt and pain of betrayal, looked beyond my own failings and those of my ex-friends. I did help them find a path toward happiness, even as I might assist a stranger. And then I stepped off their path and onto my own.

I now look forward to the future, open to possibility. I now seek constructive and mutually beneficial relationships, tempered with consideration for the ephemeral nature of all things.

What price did I pay for personal growth and greater awareness? Loss of naiveté, I suppose. And, perhaps, my toll includes the reality of these painful, unwelcome memories, locked away forever in a remote corner of my soul.

Jan Kraus had a successful career in Information Technology. From 2012–2014, as Adjunct Professor at St. Louis Community College, in partnership with Stanford University and the Bill and Melinda Gates Foundation, she authored several modules for the first issue of the Carnegie Mellon Healthcare IT Foundations–OLI course. Jan has even more fun now. She writes, draws, and paints. As a singer/songwriter, her song "Space Age" was introduced in the 2019 *It's Time to Write a Song* album, produced by Kevin Renick. Jan's 250-word-or-less Sci-Fi stories were read at the Geisel Library's "Short Tales from the Mothership" events in 2020, 2021, and 2022. Her short story appears in the 2023 St. Louis Writer's Guild Anthology; her poem illustrated with her painting is in the 2023 St. Louis County Library Poetry Anthology; and her flash fiction story illustrated with her drawing appears in the St. Louis Public Library Central Writers Group 2023 ZINE.

Jaqueline Larrecou-Whipple

A Journey of Hope

Sitting in the circle, all I could hear was my own voice in my head, "How did I end up here?" I was thirty-eight and saw nothing to show for it. Financially ruined despite having a successful career, which I had now lost, I also faced a court order barring contact with my beautiful son. I had lost my house and car and held only the barest of relationships with my family. In fact, I held even less of a relationship with myself. I heard people talk about hitting rock bottom and wondered, "Is this it? Is *this* what rock bottom feels like?"

As my turn came up to check in about my emotional state, I looked around the circle and into the eyes of the other women who had shared their true feelings. After two weeks of saying I was fine, my feelings exploded and I yelled, "I feel angry, disappointed, and scared!"

It was time for me to get real, with myself and the others in the residential treatment facility. I only had ninety days, and I'd already wasted the first fourteen. I needed to get raw and truthful with myself.

After twenty-four years of drinking and using drugs, more days than not I was tired of being tired. Lost and no longer holding the pieces of my life together, I finally found the strength to say out loud, "I *am* an alcoholic and addict." In twelve-step programs, that statement is step one. I didn't know it at the time, but saying those words out loud changed the trajectory of my life.

My substance abuse started innocently enough, as it does for many of us, and in my first year of high school. The house parties on weekends always included a keg of beer and occasionally some weed to smoke. Sometimes such parties could be on weekdays after school when friends' parents were away.

I didn't realize at the time, but looking back now on those early years, there were signs I was predisposed to addiction. Once I started, I never wanted to stop. Not wanting to miss out on any fun, I was always the last to go to sleep. Most of my friends didn't really enjoy the tase of alcohol and drank just to get buzzed. Not me. I drank because I liked the taste of alcohol.

Elementary school was always hard for me. Dyslexic and undiagnosed until my junior year of high school, I was challenged to keep up in all my classes at the competitive private schools I attended, yet still managed to do well enough. I played sports—not very well, but it's easy to make the team when your class is small. Being chubby when younger, I was teased a lot. With a smile on my face, I laughed it off and pretended it didn't bother me. Now I can say it hurt. It hurt a lot and stayed with me into my adult life.

Going into high school, I lost some weight and came into my own. After a few sports injuries and a few car accidents, my doctors prescribed pain killers and muscle relaxers. A serious car accident just as my senior year began meant sports were no longer an option. Instead, stuck in physical therapy and prescribed more pills, I couldn't workout, I couldn't maintain my schoolwork, and started regaining weight. I needed help, first to keep up my grades, as required by my college acceptance offer, and second because there was no way I was going to become that chubby little girl again. I found the perfect answer in cocaine.

I saw cocaine as a miracle! It enabled me to stay awake to study, and because I didn't want to eat I started losing weight again, even while still drinking. Only a handful of my friends knew, and I never used coke with them. For me, coke wasn't to party; it was to help me cope and get through the day. I was now eighteen and on my way to college as a full-blown addict and alcoholic.

I was deep into a vicious cycle of days that began with snorting a line of coke to wake up, followed by a drink because I was too wired, another line to stay awake, and then more drinking so I could sleep. There was always a line left on my nightstand at bedtime, for the next morning. Already deep into the insanity of addiction, that cycle became my daily routine for many years to come.

Believing my substance abuse was invisible to others, I rationalized, "I don't have a problem; I have a full-time job, I pay my bills, I have a car, and I have a roof over my head." Until one day, all of that was gone.

The two years leading up to my recovery were the darkest of my life. Looking back, I have no regrets about that part of my story because without the downward spiral to hit bottom, I'd never have found help.

There were days I thought might be my last. My son was so young… would he even remember me? What stories would people tell him about me? Some days I just wanted to go to sleep and not wake up. Too ashamed to even look in the mirror, I suspect I'd no longer have recognized myself anyway.

Some may wonder that I have no regrets. The secret is knowing that everything I put myself through (yes, I have stopped blaming everyone else) has made me who I am today. I have made amends to those I hurt by my choices along the way, except for a handful who were called home before I was able to and with whom I have made peace after years of growth. There *are* times I think, "Look at all the years I wasted!" but quickly remind myself they weren't wasted but are a part of what made me who I am. Those years helped make me strong, and without them I may not have learned to live the life I want and deserve. Those twenty-four years gave me one of life's greatest gifts: hope.

January 31, 2011, was my first day of sobriety, but back then I couldn't even put together the seventy-two hours required before check-in by the treatment facility. When asked, "Have you used any illegal substances or had any alcohol in the last seventy-two hours?" I lied with a giant smile on my face, "No!" I was high as a kite and not able to stop fidgeting. I am forever grateful that they turned a blind eye, completed my paperwork, and transported me to my new home for the next ninety days.

If they hadn't, to the bottom of a long waiting list I would have been sent, and the entire process would be restarted. With the overabundance of drugs I was taking, I'm not sure I'd have lived through the added months to get back to the top of that list. They took a chance on giving me the opportunity. For ninety days I had nothing to worry about but learning the tools to create a strong foundation of recovery. And I still wield those tools every day!

I am fine with saying I am an alcoholic and addict and will be for the rest of my life. Balance arrived in my life and my relationships when I stopped living a life of insanity, expecting sane outcomes. Forgiving myself allowed me to love myself. Every day I remember where I came from so that I am not tempted to go back. Yes, the urge to drink or use drugs has gone. Living life one day at a time is manageable for me, so that is what I continue to do. It is the foundation for me, living a life in recovery: forgive myself for the past, live in the present day, and don't worry about tomorrow; it hasn't even happened yet!

I am a dream catcher who continues to raise my own bar each time I reach it! If telling my story helps just one addict or alcoholic admit to themselves that they need help, then living my story out loud is worth it! I am proof that help is out there if you ask and are willing and ready to accept it.

I thank all those other recovering alcoholics and addicts who came before me, and I hope to inspire those who come after me. I remember those who didn't make it and keep them in my heart. I owe my life to a wonderful man, Jim Stansberry, who believed in me and so many others. He has helped so many of us alcoholics and addicts find our way, living the Twelve Steps.

All you need to succeed in life is hope. And hope comes from other people believing in you, even when you can't believe in yourself. I believe in you. I believe in second chances. I believe in change, and I believe anyone can change if they have support and hope. In the words of my husband, "If no one told you today they love you, I just did."

Jaqueline Larrecou-Whipple is a mother, wife, executive assistant, transformational coach, mentor, dream catcher, hope champion, and recovering alcoholic and drug addict. She is a huge San Francisco Giants and 49ers fan and roots for the Fighting Irish!

Jenny Gaume

Aren't You Embarrassed?

My life is not unique. I am not wealthy or famous. I do not own a big business, nor have I invented anything cool that has become a household name. Instead, my life is a journey of twists, turns, dead ends, and rerouting, which provided avenues to learn a few valuable insights. One of the most empowering lessons so far is that the weight of embarrassment is garbage. It is a stinking, heavy burden. Do not journey with it in the trunk. Leave that rubbish in the bin.

Everyone has embarrassing moments. For instance, in a high school sex-ed class, the teacher asked for the definition of premature ejaculation. I had read the lesson, and I eagerly raised my hand…only to realize that I did not want to give the correct answer aloud in front of my peers. I stuttered something unrecognizable and then pretended not to know the answer. I heard snickering behind me and felt the heat on my neck. I wanted to disappear!

Then there was the time I lost control of a tray of five strawberry margaritas, all over a lady at Red Lobster. Everyone stared and gasped; some laughed, and others just watched in horror as the sticky, red, freezing slush splashed all over her and me. She got a free meal, and I got sent home.

I also got lost on the land navigation test when I was in the Army, and all the sergeants laughed at me. I had to do the entire test again on another day while my classmates enjoyed some time off. They laughed at me, too, when I returned to the barracks that evening. So much for *esprit de corps*!

My navigation skills are still crummy. One time I accidentally drove the wrong direction in Japan, where they drive on the left. Thankfully, I maneuvered to the shoulder and turned around safely. A few locals witnessed my mistake and shook their heads disapprovingly. How embarrassing!

Yet all of these events passed, and I am reasonably confident that I am the only person who recalls them. Well, except maybe the lady who wore strawberry margaritas home from dinner.

But looking back on my journey of life, all these embarrassing moments are now inconsequential.

However, there are some bigger embarrassments that stick: the most imperfect moments. They are difficult, if not impossible, to hide. In one of my biggies, it seemed that everyone knew my business and had something to say about it. And one particular someone's message took me to a new understanding of embarrassment.

I started dating a man who liked me and, in fact, fell in love with me. All was bliss, or so I thought. This new sweetie saw me and my five fabulous kids, my successful career, and my primarily level-headed self and asked, "You have been married twice and divorced twice; aren't you embarrassed?"

I began gnawing at his judgmental question, determined to get myself into a better place, because it triggered some discomfort. Honestly, how dare he? While I was embarrassed, I did not appreciate the question, and I suddenly understood that not only was I embarrassed, I was *supposed* to be embarrassed! Why did his evaluation of me hurt so badly? Why did I let it, and why did I agree with him? It was like he wanted me to be embarrassed and voice it out loud. The message I received was that, while he was happy I was available, I should carry the weight of embarrassment. Divorce is hard enough without others expecting you to exist in a state of oppressive embarrassment and shame. That relationship ended, and then, later, in another one, my beau and I talked about marriage and he said to me, "I have been divorced twice; you have been divorced twice. Aren't you embarrassed?"

There it was again, dang it! Fire lit; game on!

Embarrass is a funny word. I used to think that it was akin to having a bare a$$! To me, that would be super em-bare-ass-ing, but, in fact, I learned that this word is much more interesting than that. The prefix *em* is from the Latin, which means to "put in," and the rest comes from the Portuguese *baraça*, the word for "noose." No wonder that sometimes just recalling some of my more embarrassing moments can cause heat to rise through my body—especially in my neck—my pulse to elevate, and adrenaline to pump. My fight-or-flight responses engage, lighting my brain stem on fire. *Please, someone, cut me down from this noose so I can run.*

Unlike most fleeting moments of embarrassment, somehow divorce, the "big D" word, lingers… and it hurts. Like most women, I did not want a divorce, but it was necessary. A noose hung around my neck, holding a big pendant called embarrassment. I dragged it everywhere I went. Whether people knew me or not, I dreaded revealing my divorce. It was a heavy burden.

What is the truth? The truth is, yes, I was married twice and divorced twice, but does that mean I failed? More linguistic research helped me learn that the word divorce comes from the Latin word *divortium,* which means separation, and that doesn't seem to be such a bad word. What if I said that my first husband and I went different ways after bringing into this world five amazing humans whom we both love very much and who are all successful and well adjusted? Is that a failure? I should say not!

When I look back, I see many beautiful years. We were kids, and we started our adult lives together and enjoyed many good times. We chose to end our marriage. We had different life goals and desires. We disagreed, we grew apart, we separated.

My second marriage was super fun but not without challenges. This man taught me that I was strong, beautiful, and deserved so much in this life. He bought me my first string of pearls because I had no jewelry, and he told me *every woman should have pearls*. He surprised me with evenings out and trips to exotic places, and expanded my worldview. He supported me in pursuing my master's degree and praised my efforts. However, we also found that our paths trended in different directions, so we chose to part. Does that sound like a failure, or the end of a chapter?

I admit, at first divorcing did feel like a failure, but I learned that I can frame these events in my life for my empowerment. I can flip the narrative. I started reading self-help books, especially those with peer-reviewed research. I listened to podcasts and embedded new ideas into my subconscious. Because I learned that mindset is at the heart of every transformation, I became super intentional about my life and my thoughts.

Finally, I realized that the question "Aren't you embarrassed?" is not about what others think of me, but it *invokes* what I think of myself. The truth was, I thought a lot of myself; yet that self-worth coexisted with a perpetual state of embarrassment. I knew I was a good person, but I let my divorces define me…for a time.

The question "Aren't you embarrassed?," which I perceived to be an indictment, first messed with my head and held me back from living life on my terms. In retrospect, I am thankful for this question that helped me break free of embarrassment and pursue my dreams on my terms. Rather than allow judgment to hold me in that noose, I liberated myself from the garbage of embarrassment.

Ultimately, the decision to free myself from embarrassment was a choice. I decided to explore my story and shape how it influenced my personhood. I took my biggest embarrassment and made it my biggest strength. If I could go back in time to that question from both of those boyfriends, "Aren't you embarrassed?," I would be ready with a different response. I would say confidently, "I am who I am because of all that I have lived. You fell in love with the woman I am today; why would you want to change anything about who I am or what I have experienced?" Mic drop.

I am now in the driver's seat of my story. Divorce did not define me, but it helped shape the strong woman I am today. The people I most care about in the world—my children—are proud of me, and theirs are the only opinions I care about.

Now I am off to a new adventure in my life, and I love it. I took my lifelong passion for health and wellness to the professional level. As a certified health and wellness coach, I help women break through their self-limiting mindsets—like my embarrassments—to achieve the health and wellness they deserve. Overcoming the struggles of embarrassment and insecurities left by my divorces took me to a place where I am skilled and driven to help others on their journey to ideal health and wellness.

I am happily on the other side of hanging in that noose of embarrassment, ready to help others, free of the limits of my past. Now I advise women: do not exist in embarrassment and do not let your unmet dreams of optimal health hold you in a noose. My mission today is to empower women to achieve all their dreams through their health and wellness. I advise them all that, if they have lived some embarrassing stuff and someone reminds them of it with that "Aren't you embarrassed" hook, simply respond, "No, I am not embarrassed. I am a perfect imperfection, in the flesh."

Jenny Gaume is a certified women's health and wellness coach. She helps women break through limiting beliefs to achieve the optimal health they want and deserve. Originally from Alton, Illinois, and an Army Veteran, she has five adult children who are the joy of her life, two little dogs, and an occasional foster dog. Her passions are her children, dogs, fitness, nutrition, cooking, reading, learning, chocolate, roller coasters, and traveling. Jenny holds a Bachelor of Music Education degree from Pacific Lutheran University and a Master of Science degree in Physical Education, Health, and Recreation from Emporia University.

Jess Beeson

Damn It! I Forgot My Bra!

"Damn it! I forgot my bra!" I said, in perhaps a slightly too-whiny tone for a grown woman. It's not often a hospital emergency room staff (including the surgeon) is left speechless, but I've pulled off this feat more often than most. I watched as the expressions of the two nurses and the surgeon danced through a myriad of emotions…and I waited (somewhat impatiently) for them to catch up. Their expressions turned from looks of shock and confusion to ones of wary compassion. Perhaps they understood I was in a state of shock but were still contemplating sending me to the white wing with padded walls and buckled jackets. It wouldn't be the first time I'd made people in the medical field question my sanity.

"Mrs. Beeson," one of the nurses said as she set her hand on my arm. "Do you understand what we are telling you?"

I am a strong, independent adult woman who can handle a lot of serious situations and can communicate effectively within these situations, so when I tell you I tried *really* hard *not* to roll my eyes, I promise that I *did* try. However, judging from the downturned corners of her mouth and the annoyed look in her eyes, the nurse with her hand on my arm was not amused.

"Mrs. Beeson?" she asked again.

I took a deep breath and tried to remember what my therapist had taught me about counting to ten as I inhaled and exhaled. I closed my eyes and heard her clear, melodic, Disneyesque voice say, *When you feel the fear and panic rise, it's time to breathe. Start by closing your eyes. Now, breathe in…One, two, buckle my shoe. Three, four, shut the door…*

"Mrs. Beeson?" the nurse tried a third time as the second nurse approached me warily. There was no way they would know that I was singing nursing rhymes in my head while I tried to remember how to count to ten for a breathing exercise. They probably thought I was going to pass out and become their next patient.

"Yes," I replied, irritated that neither woman was understanding the predicament that *I* was experiencing about forgetting my bra. I tried to remember if I still had that stretchy one that I'd taken off while sitting at a stoplight last week because the tag was driving me nuts. I'd have to run out and check after I found out which room he was in. "I understand, but…"

The surgeon cut me off. "Mrs. Beeson. Your husband is dying. We've done everything we can do, but the intestine has completely twisted in a way that's preventing blood flow to his other organs. We have tried every intervention for the clots in his chest and lack of blood to vital areas, but his body isn't responding. He is no longer breathing on his own and will likely not make it through the night."

I glanced at the clock. 12:37 a.m. "Well, good thing the sun doesn't rise until seven thirty. That means you all have seven hours to figure out how to wake his ass up." The almost nonexistent filter my beautiful (but sometimes inappropriate) ADHD brain owns but rarely likes to use was clearly on OFF. If you are someone who also responds to stressful situations with sarcasm, then you probably understand my response. If your face also lacks a filtration device, consider recording it as you read this next part, or ask someone to describe your reaction in the next few seconds. I promise it will give you both a good laugh.

"I am very sorry for your loss, Mrs. Beeson," the surgeon said crisply. Then he turned and walked straight out of the room.

In this moment, I understood three things:
1. That surgeon had decided my husband was going to die before I even left home that night.
2. I really needed to order more bras!
3. It *wasn't* his time. Have you ever gotten that weird feeling when you just *know* something? Call it a God-wink. Call it a spiritual tap on the shoulder. Call it a one-way ticket to Crazy Town. Call it whatever you like, but this intuition has been spot-on too often in my life to ignore it. Jeremy's time will come someday, but in that moment I *knew* it wouldn't be that night. I also knew that Jeremy needed help coming back to us, and if that doctor wasn't going to do it, then I sure as hell would.

"Mrs. Beeson..." the first nurse started to say.

"I'd like to see my husband now, please," I said, standing and looking for which direction they had taken him.

"Of course. I just want to warn you. You can talk to him, but he won't be able to hear you or respond. He has also been intubated, which means that—"

"I know what intubated means," I said, cutting her off. "This isn't the first time I've gotten the 'Come Say Goodbye to Your Husband' call, and I'm sure it won't be the last," I snapped. I still feel guilty about how short I was with her, but I was *exhausted*. Being married to a man who had a liver transplant following liver cancer at the ripe old age of twenty-six meant that we'd spent our fair share of nights in the hospital, and that was *before* parenthood. At that time, we also had a ten-month-old baby girl at home who was teething, not sleeping, and trying to give her mother heart attacks on a daily basis…*and* the surgeon charged with saving my husband's life had just quit. He had quit on Jeremy. He had quit on me, and he had quit on our daughter.

The nurse showed me to Jeremy's room. Once there, I just stood in the doorway and watched him.

I watched his chest as it rose with the respirator.

Up and down. Up and down. Up and down.

I listened to the steady beep of the heart-rate monitor as it read his rhythm.

Beep…beep…beep.

Then I started thinking about the bra that may (or may not) still be in my back seat. I know, I know! You thought this was going to be a weepy-all-in-the-feels retelling of the night my husband died, but I told you: I *knew* tonight wasn't his last night.

Stepping to his bedside, I pressed the "silence" button on the machine, ending the irritating beeping. Then I carefully laid down next to this loving, kind, miracle of a human being I was blessed to marry. I held his hand, placed my ear above his heart so I could listen to *it* beating instead of the machine…and I talked. I talked about our life together, and the silly things our daughter did that day. I talked about all the silly things *I* did that day, how much I respected him, admired him, and loved him. I talked about how I really needed to order more of those bras on Amazon. I talked for hours…until he came back to me.

I was just telling him he needed to get out of his comfort zone when it came to dancing, so he could dance at our daughter's wedding, when he *jerked*. Not a little twitch of his eyes or a little squeeze in his hand; the man damn-near tossed me off the bed.

The next hour was sheer chaos with nurses and doctors trying to figure out why a "dead man" was now trying to pull out his own tubes.

I knew I looked like a hot mess, and I knew I didn't have my bra, but I didn't care. Jeremy had come back to me, and that was all that mattered.

I get asked all the time how we've gotten through so many experiences like this, and it really comes down to these five tools for overcoming trauma:

1. DON'T FORGET YOUR BRA! Just kidding…sorta. Dress how *you* want. Your clothes are a reflection of *you* and have a huge impact on how you feel.
2. LAUGH. Find as many moments as you can to laugh, so that when the hard things come (and they will), you have enough joy to outshine the pain.
3. LIVE FREELY. Live the life *you* want to live. We never have as much time as we want. Don't waste it.
4. HAVE HOPE. Never give up on hope. Hope brings you back from the edge of giving up. Hope is what keeps us going, and hope is what will ultimately save you.
5. LOVE. Love those around you and let them love you back. Lean on them when you need them. They are there because they love *you*.

   Take time to show love but *make* time to *feel* it…and remember to love yourself too.

I hope reading this helps you, whether you have experienced something similarly traumatic or a different kind of trauma. Know that I feel your pain. I see you. I hear you. We all have different stories, and we all have to go through hard things. You *are* stronger than you think you are, but just because you *can* do it alone doesn't mean you *have* to.

XOXO

-Jess B.

P.S. I still haven't ordered more bras, by the way. Maybe I can get Jeremy to put them in the Amazon cart when he orders trash bags…

Jess Beeson is Founder and CEO of Willow Tree Tutoring, LLC and Jess B., LLC. She has been with her husband for eighteen years, and they share a beautiful daughter. After receiving her Bachelor of Arts degree in Middle School English Education from Lindenwood University, she spent eight years in the public school system before starting her tutoring company in 2012, combining academics, stress management, self-confidence, and organizational and test-taking skills. In 2022, she founded Jess B. LLC, creating the "Be You. Be Free." program, to integrate neuroscience, entrepreneurship, and neurodiversity. The program is effective, powerful, and an inspirational journey for those who want to understand the *what*, *why*, and *how* of overcoming all the hard things in life.

Jessica Grace

Self-Love: The Simplest Solution

Can you imagine standing in front of a full-length mirror, looking at yourself and thinking, "Wow, I love how I look!" without a hint of doubt or sarcasm? I predict that would be a big stretch for most women.

I can confidently say I'm there. Actually, I'm *more* than there. I can look at myself in the mirror and think, "Holy whoa, I'm hot. Like, *hot*-hot." I did not start there, though. It took years and years of positive self-talk to undo stories I retold in my head, supported by society, random men and women, movies, posters, TV shows, and family and friends.

If you are overweight, or have ever been overweight, you know people *love* to tell you about it. Most of the time their judgment is masked behind "I'm worried about your health." Some of the *un*-cool things people said to me included: "If you lost weight, you'd look just like Elizabeth Taylor," "You'd be a ten if you lost weight," "You're so beautiful, but you still have a little weight left to lose," "Do you really think you need all that food?," and so many more through the years. I heard these ignorant comments and fought off others' obsession with my weight from the age of eight (think WeightWatchers and the Atkin's diet in middle school).

Results of the relentless judgment included the emotional exhaustion of low self-confidence, mixing with physical weakness from my obsession with fad dieting. Every Monday, my life was going to change because

I would finally stick with whatever new diet I was trying. Every week, I failed before the next weekend was over and prayed for the will power to do better the next week. I hated my body, believed I would never find a romantic partner, and lived in constant disappointment with myself.

How did I go from all that self-loathing to loving my body unconditionally? My not-so-secret medicine was simply a "little bit" of self-love and acceptance.

Until that shift, I deeply learned unhelpful lessons from several influential women in my life, as I watched them stand in front of the mirror, grab the fat around their middle, and let out a disgusted "ugh." What girl child has *not* witnessed this or a similar scene? Without realizing it, I was learning that all that matters is how our bodies look, absorbing the idea that being skinny was the only goal. Seeing the women I loved and looked up to model this mindset taught me that having fat on my body is disgusting. The belief wasn't conscious, but it was heavily reinforced with pressures from family, community, and the media.

Years ago, TV and movie characters bigger than a size eight were only cast in comedic, supporting roles. Never as the main star, or the love interest, always recreating narratives that affirmed only beautiful, thin women (with great hair) get the hunky guy and live happily ever after. As a little girl obsessed with princess movies, I learned that a man and a tiny waist should be my only goals, as signposts on the road to true happiness.

For more than ten years, starting in fourth grade and continuing into my early twenties, I thought about my weight all the time, carried armloads of guilt for failed attempts to lose it, and always felt I was not trying hard enough . . . at most of life.

Finally, I was done. Exhausted, sad, defeated, and done. I accidentally started my self-love journey, completely changed my mindset, and gained happiness beyond anything I'd imagined.

The mindset change that quite literally changed my life came from self-help books. I hit inspirational books hard! They shared ideas completely foreign to me, such as loving myself, forgiving myself, and silently, privately forgiving people who wronged me. One surprising new lesson was that it is OK to love my body, even if it is not "perfect" according to society's standards. I started thinking things like, "Wow, what if I didn't hate my body?"

Oddly, I felt terrible even *thinking* that. Surely if I stopped hating myself, I'd "let myself go." But hating myself was not working either. If hating our bodies worked, we would all look like supermodels.

Something had to change, so I started with a little daily self-love. This extremely simple practice changed everything. Looking in the mirror, I said aloud, "I love you." All day long, I thought to myself, "I love you."

The first time I tried it, I could not look myself in the eyes while I did it. I did not believe myself. I knew I did not love myself. Fortunately, when you say something enough, you *start* to believe it. I was doing many types of affirmations, but this is the one that made the biggest difference. Simply saying "I love you" into the mirror as you brush your hair is a fantastic place to start if you, too, are looking to add a little self-love to your life. It sounds so basic, but the mindset gurus are right! We really can change our thoughts and feelings—if we just "fake it 'til we make it!"

I worked on growing my self-love for long enough that, by my late twenties, Instagram was in full swing. I had never seen plus-size women represented positively before. I was so inspired by new influencers like Tess Holliday, Ashley Graham, Jen Taylor, and Liza Mae Frick, I decided I wanted to start sharing my daily outfits online too.

When I first started posting pictures of my outfits, I was too ashamed to add the *#plussize* category of connected visibility. That term was still so negative in my mind, even after all those years of self-love! But I shared my images anyway. As a plus-size woman, posting my outfits daily was revolutionary in those years. Other women would inbox me, "I just wish I had your confidence." And I thought to myself, "To what? Wear a dress?"

But each message was also a reminder of how much more we, as a society, still need to do to promote self-acceptance and *body positivity*, a now-common term that means our worth is not determined by our body's size or shape. Not by how we look or how much we weigh, nor even by the balance in our savings account. Body-positive people know we are enough *just as we are*.

Recently, I've lost quite a bit of weight, and those who knew me before often ask, "Don't you just feel *so much better*?" My answer is always, "No, I don't." I can run up a flight of stairs faster, don't worry about an airplane seatbelt buckling, and enjoy having a wider selection of clothing easily available when I shop. I don't worry about half the things I used to about my physical ability or being comfortable. So in those respects, yes, I do feel much better.

However, I am still the same person. I feel exactly the same in every other aspect of my self. I still love the same, work very hard at my job, and have the same friends. My thoughts and ideas are the same. Through the continuing practice of self-love, I had come to love my body so much even before I lost weight that now I feel a teeny bit sad for those who assume "feeling better" means *happier with my body*. I am sympathetic, guessing they are in the spot I was in ten years ago, with my self-worth tied to my weight and how my body looked. But I know I am the same person now as when I was a hundred pounds heavier, and will still be the same loving, hardworking, friendly person if I gain back every one of those pounds plus a hundred more.

When I signed on the dotted line, committing to write this chapter, I knew it scared me, and that was good reason to do it. This past year,

I have more often said yes to things that scare me. I didn't realize how much sharing my story meant to me until I finished writing the first raw draft. If this story helps one woman, I'm happy. If this story helps one mother see a way to raise her little girl to grow up loving rather than hating her body, I am *extra* happy.

I am so excited to share my story. My power of self-love for overcoming my sense of having no worth, no value, may sound trivial. You might think, "Self-acceptance and self-love…so what?" But, for me, self-love broke generational habits. For me, being brave enough to love myself and speak about it to other people has been, well, everything.

Jessica Grace is a licensed esthetician, acne clearing specialist, and self-proclaimed expert on self-love, located in Godfrey, Illinois. She loves inspiring women to embrace the skin they're in and accept themselves, no matter their shape or size. She shares her life with one pup named Maggie, and loves spending time with friends and family.

Kathryn Malloy

You Are Stronger Than You Seem

"Hey, girls, why don't you run inside and say hi to Grandma? I'll go home to gather what we need." Little did I know this simple statement was the beginning of the end…

I went to our home and gathered a few things for the girls, then to my bedroom to gather what I would need for the night and the next day. My gut told me we needed to stay somewhere "safer" that night.

Suddenly I was attacked, but not by a stranger; by my husband, Dave. He demanded money and, dangerously flailing a knife, pushed me down on the air mattress we now slept on, since he sold our bed to support his drug habit. I had no money; he had stolen every penny I had made for weeks. I don't remember exactly what I said, but I got him to stop forcing himself on me and terrifying me with the knife. That's when he told me I needed to take him somewhere. I reminded him I could not leave without the girls, and he said he would go get them, then asked to meet him in the driveway.

I agreed but only to get out of the situation. As soon as he was about halfway to his parents' house next door, I drove directly across the grass and ran inside. His parents saw my disheveled look and questioned what happened. I gave a short version as Dave was still coming toward us. He had now begun asking his dad to take him wherever to get him out of there. And he did…

Once they were gone, I walked back to my house and was greeted by the county police department. They were coming to check on me, as I had an ex parte order filed to protect us from Dave. His mom and I shared with the police what had happened, and they left in search of him, to arrest him for violating the restraining order.

Once the officer left, I continued to my house, while yet another vehicle pulled in. When I asked if I could help, he advised me that the house was being foreclosed on and I had until Saturday at noon to gather all my things. This was Thursday evening.

Our marriage did not start this way. We met shortly after I graduated high school. He was the first guy to really pay me any attention, and what girl does not want that? We were together all the time…night and day! He was wonderful to me, we traveled, and hung out with friends and family all the time!

Less than one year later, we moved in together. Within six months we were married, and life was wonderful. He never let anyone speak poorly of me or around me; he was my protector. Just short of three years after we married, we welcomed our first child, Shauna. She was (and still is) a blessing. Carefree and easygoing, she slept through the night from the start. My husband's friends even loved coming over to play with her.

Little did I realize he was jealous of the attention I was now giving her rather than him. I am not even sure when things truly shifted, or if I recognized it. Within twenty-two months of having Shauna, we welcomed our second daughter, Ali. She was another beautiful baby, but I think the stress building during my pregnancy was passed along to her. I believe she still carries it to this day. Before I returned to work from maternity leave,

Dave admitted himself to the ER for heart issues, but their assessment determined nothing to be wrong.

Looking back now, I recognize that this is when things really started to fail for him. We had two beautiful girls, he had a great job, and I was working my way up as well!

Yet over the next two and a half years, life as we knew it started to unravel. He quit going to work on a regular basis and ended up spending more "time on the bench" (a union term for more time sitting rather than working). That meant no income from him. While I continued to work and take the girls to child care every day, we were short on income to cover our bills every month. He always found a way to make it work, until he could no longer support his multiple addictions *and* the bills, so the bills became secondary.

One day I came home to find our bed gone; another day to find the TV disconnected and ready for sale. One evening, while I was home alone with the girls, a strange man knocked on the sliding glass door and asked for Dave. Though Dave was not there, this man made it clear that Dave owed him money and he would return for it. I was terrified but unsure what to do. I didn't want my friends and family to know the extent of what was going on. Would you?

But then it became increasingly obvious. We would go to gatherings together and he would leave me there. We attended a party during which all of the beer ran out. Someone began a collection for more, Dave offered to go get it, but he had no plan to return. The partygoers started coming to me asking, "Where is he?" and "Where is my money?" Another time, we went to someone's home and he just left me there! I had to find a ride home, and when I did, I found him there, but he had hidden his truck behind the house. When I went inside, he called me a whore because a guy (a mutual friend) had brought me home!

He never raised his hand or hit me, but boy did those words, as well as the keys and the coffee table he threw at me, hurt! In my heart, I believed that I could fix him. I was by his side for rehabilitation, including urging him to make the decision to go to rehab. At one point he did spend a few weeks in a nearby rehabilitation center. The center allowed him to come home for one evening so he could attend his grandparents' anniversary party. When I took him back, the rehab required a drug test. Needless to say, he did not pass. You cannot help someone who doesn't want help.

After that night he pulled the knife, within a few days we moved out, with the county police department supporting and protecting us. Once everything was loaded, the girls and I headed to Kansas City to stay with my mom until things could calm down and we could return. Fortunately, I had a wonderful and supportive supervisor at work who allowed me the time I needed.

During our time in Kansas City, Dave decided he wanted us back. In phone calls, he threatened my dad, sister, and uncle. They involved the police departments in their cities, who were already familiar with the situation. It was determined that my family should go to an undisclosed location, where Dave could not find them, which meant they had to be away from their homes for a while.

Then Dave walked into a grocery store with a sawed-off shotgun in hand, requesting change for the payphone (in those pre-cell phone days). He was so strung out—he told me later that he had gotten into intravenous drugs at this point—that he didn't realize he was still carrying the weapon. The grocery store personnel called the police, who initiated a manhunt and finally caught him several hours later.

The girls and I returned to our hometown, hoping to rebuild, but we had nowhere to stay. Finally, we worked out an arrangement to live in my great grandmother's home. Now, to get Shauna enrolled in school and return to normal…only to find a mess of barriers in our way! Dave had taken the girls' birth certificates and social security cards, our new home was not in the best district, *and* I had no proof of residency.

And then…it all worked out. Other family members allowed us to use their address and vouched that we were living with them to get Shauna enrolled and in class only one day after school started! We had a safe place to live, Shauna was in school, and Ali was going to my sister's for child care. Hallelujah! I really could go back to work to start getting our lives into a new normal!

What I learned through this experience is to remain strong. I honestly don't know where I would be if not for my daughters. To this day, twenty years later, they are a significant part of my strength. They believe in me, support me, and are behind me in every way. When they were young, I was their strength; but as they have grown and matured, they are definitely mine. I owe them more than they will ever understand. We will always be close; they will always be my best friends. When you find yourself in what seems an impossible situation, when all the doors seem to be closed, you can find a strength within you that you never knew was there. And your loved ones, supporting you, make you all the more likely to succeed.

Kathryn Malloy, who prefers Katie, was born and raised in Foristell, Missouri, and still resides there today. Among many roles, she is first and foremost a mom and—she likes to think, a pretty good one. She loves to create fun memories with those she loves, and typically will be doing wearing pink; it is her happy color. She is a killer at sales, and her passion drives her to make the most of each day, getting people as comfortable in their homes and businesses as possible.

Katie Fry

She Believed She Could…So She Did

I pressed my head against the seat and squeezed my eyes shut, wishing the world would stop spinning. How? Why? What just happened? My heart was pounding and the lump in my throat refused to leave, but the tears wouldn't fall. I was in a state of shock. I started the vehicle and looked behind me before backing out, catching a glimpse of all my belongings—the belongings that I had carefully curated to make a home away from home, a place I felt safe and comfortable. A place I imagined I would spend the next twenty-five years.

Just the week before, my friend and mentor leaned in the doorway of that safe place. We laughed, joked, and talked about whether I wanted to pursue a new certification or a doctorate. I was comfortable…and comfortable usually means I need to move forward. "I can't be stagnant," I said, and he laughed. "God knows you'll find something to do to challenge yourself," he replied. "Sometimes I wish God would just tell us what we're supposed to do. Like smack us in the head and say, 'Hey…this is your next step,'" I responded.

I could not have predicted the smack that was coming.

The world was in the middle of a global pandemic. I am a nurse practitioner.

Our rural Midwest community was not hit hard, but we in healthcare were still affected. I was the first provider to enter the makeshift tent for potential patients. I was the first to see a test swab from a patient come back with a positive result, and the first to risk exposure to this potentially deadly virus. It was the first time in my nearly twenty-year career that I wondered whether I was still called to nursing. The face of healthcare was already changing, and the pandemic kicked that change into high gear. My priority was always my patients, but it was getting harder and harder to hold on to patient relationships and still be in alignment with the corporate requirements of the healthcare system. Yet I knew I couldn't ever leave. This role in nursing is all I have ever wanted, and it was as much a part of who I am as breathing.

So that glimpse of my back seat full of my life set my heart pounding in my chest. I was hurt. I was embarrassed. I was stunned. I was betrayed. I never saw this coming. My hands gripped the steering wheel, running through the conversation I had just unknowingly been invited into. I looked at the clock…it had been forty-five minutes.

In just forty-five minutes, I had seen my first—and it turned out, only—patient of the day, and then was called into a meeting where my entire world turned upside down.

I took a deep breath and exited the parking lot for the last time.

At the pandemic's start, healthcare workers were deemed heroes; hearts adorned homes and businesses to support us as we walked headfirst into the storm, protected only by reused masks and thin paper gowns. Our administration told us we were in this together as we faced unprecedented challenges and changes. We had to pivot on the fly and be flexible. We saw patients in their cars. We learned about telehealth and created new protocols in a matter of days…all while hearing the horrors of what our colleagues were experiencing in larger cities. Our hallways and exam rooms were empty. It was eerie and felt like the calm before a storm. For a year, we navigated a new kind of healthcare. We listened to daily updates from governors and the surgeon general. We listened to local authorities and adjusted everything about how we ran our daily operations.

As the pandemic progressed, we continued to do more with less, but our exam rooms became more volatile. Politics and the news intermingled with ever-changing guidelines, making our offices feel more like a battle zone than a safe space. We faced skepticism at best and abuse at worst. Healthcare jobs were being eliminated at a never-before-seen rate, and the stability of the field came into question. I understood this to be the case nationwide. No one was hiring nurse practitioners. We were being let go.

I was being let go.

The conversation swirled around me. I was not sure I was following the words being tossed out by the administrators in the room. I just heard bits and pieces as my brain raced to process what I was being told.

pandemic…budget…downsize…sad…sorry…

I'll cancel your afternoon appointments.

I'll help you pack your things.

What would I do? How would I rebound from this? How would I tell my husband and my kids that everything has changed? *She Believed She Could . . . So She Did.* My life's mantra. These words have played through my head in every challenging moment of my adult life. The words were etched on a sign, now stuffed in a box in the trunk. What could they mean to me now? What was left? Where do I go?

Who am I now? If not this, then what?

I tossed, turned, cried, and vented for two weeks, then decided to stop. My role in that one place did *not* define me. They took away my job, not my compassion. They did not take away my drive. They did not take away my strength. I decided then and there to be the woman I am, turn the page, and start a new chapter. This was the challenge I needed.

After all, I had said to my mentor, "I can't be stagnant."

She Believed She Could…So She Did.

I couldn't imagine starting a job in a new facility with new technology and new pandemic policies. I couldn't imagine opening myself and my family to the mercy of a corporate decision again. I couldn't imagine not overseeing my own career from this moment on. I couldn't imagine anything but opening my own practice.

The world is changing and evolving, and I must evolve too. This pandemic has brought telehealth to the forefront of the industry, and I know it already. I've done it for years. I'm good at it. I can change how we deliver health care and bring the compassion that makes me a great nurse to everyone I serve. I don't need an organization to tell me how to do my job. It's already all within me!

She Believed She Could…So She Did.

I dove headfirst into this new plan and quickly realized it was a dream come true. Fear was replaced by excitement, frustration by hope, and anger by motivation. I spent my days reading, researching, and building. I learned to write a business plan and do market research…skills I had never dreamed of adding to my repertoire! I worked in my pajamas, on the porch, or floating on a boat. I built a website and a medical practice… things I had never before considered. And *I did it.*

Questions from family and friends created doubt in my own mind: *How are you doing all this yourself? How do you know what to do?*

I don't. I'm learning as I go. It's all within me!

At times, I second-guessed this plan and feared that I was being foolish. How do you know this will be successful?

I don't, but I believe in myself and my capabilities. It's all within me!

And my mantra pushed me forward through doubt and fear. At times, it was all I had to keep me going. *She Believed She Could…So She Did.*

Do you have a deadline for it to succeed or fail?

I'm betting on myself. If I don't, who will? It's all within me!

I took a leap of faith…toward a dream that only I could see clearly. The voices around me were supportive but apprehensive. The cheers came with trepidation. The clarity was mine and mine alone. This was for me. This was to bring something more significant into the world. This journey, I had to take *for myself.*

You can probably guess that the road has not been without bumps, fear, or thoughts of maybe it's time to call it quits. In fact, there were stretches where I set this crazy dream aside and wondered if I would pick it up again. There are days when I feel selfish—that I am spending time, energy, and money on an endeavor that has no guarantee of success. There are times when I know my husband wishes I would throw in the towel and do something more traditional, more steady, and more financially stable. But every time those thoughts enter my mind, so does my mantra.

She Believed She Could…So She Did.

This new endeavor has become so much more than a job. Success has come in ways that perhaps only I can see. The business has shifted and changed; it's morphed into something entirely different than the vision I started with two years ago. And so have I.

This experience has been a masterclass in *me*, learning what is important to me as a human. Knowing how I want to show up not just in the world but *for* the world. I have learned that my needs are important, and I am the only one who can determine what I will take from this life and what I will leave behind…despite anyone else's fear, despite anyone else's questions, and despite anyone else's hesitation. Along this journey, I have learned who I am. I have learned what I am capable of. I have affirmed that everything I need is *already within me.*

I have learned to listen to the voice that believes in me the most… *my own.*

Katie Fry, MSN, APRN, FNP-C is a family nurse practitioner with twenty years of nursing experience with patients across the lifespan. Her passion in health care is holistic wellness for women, in which she supports women to prioritize themselves, understand their symptoms, and take back control of their health and wellness. She is the sole proprietor of Key Family Healthcare, PLLC. Katie is married to her high-school sweetheart, and they are parents to three awe-inspiring, near-adult daughters and three fur-babies. Katie challenges women to redefine themselves beyond the roles they play and to recognize who they are inside, holding up the model of her journey over the past two years. She defines herself as compassionate, a caregiver, intrinsically motivated, an old soul with a child's heart, and a dreamer.

Laura DeVries

What Is Your Aha! Moment?

What is an *Aha! Moment*? You'll know it when it happens because everything in your life stands still. It is a momentary jerk that has a lifelong impact. I remember my first Aha! Moment vividly. It was as if someone kicked my feet from beneath me and sucker punched me at the same time.

Like many career-driven women, my goal was climbing the corporate ladder, which resulted in an overwhelming concern about how everyone else viewed and valued me. This perspective clouded my judgment and negatively changed my priorities. And then, when my son was six, everything changed. Like many little boys, he still loved his mama and was in constant motion from sunup until sundown. After a taxing workday, I saw this innocent boy kneeling next to me as I was reading the mail, still in my post-work state of fogginess. I asked a simple question: "Jake, what are you doing?" He answered, "Huh?" with a look of confusion. I asked again, "Jacob, what are you doing?" He replied, "I'm tying my shoes." Numbly, I replied, "When did you learn to tie your shoes?" Everything around me was in slow motion. His reply was simple. "Two weeks ago, Mama. You were too busy to notice."

At that moment, with a tidal wave of emotion, I knew my life would be changed forever. That Aha! Moment triggered a passion and fueled a fire that allowed me to be more capable and accomplish more than I had ever dreamed.

What started as this Aha! Moment became the beginning of a journey. Think about that for just a moment: it is the *journey* that leads to amazing things. The journey continues today, but as it began, I was reevaluating my life and what I thought was important, and then taking it one step further—I became cognizant enough to change my path. It fueled me to start a business that I had (secretly) been dreaming about for twelve years. At that Aha! Moment, I realized that big changes were needed in my life. I would need to follow through, listen to my gut, and respect my intuition if I wanted to be the mom I knew I could be.

Starting a business was just the beginning of what became my path to mental health awareness and advocacy. I winged a lot my first year but started to pick up momentum with a commitment to work with a mentor. My first year in business has now grown to nine more. But like any good journey, it comes with extreme highs and lows, trial and error, gaining a client and losing a client…and please don't get me started on Quick-Books. Slowly the focus became clearer to me, and the fog began to lift. If you have ever considered starting a business, know it's not for the faint of heart. It took *grit* and believing that I had the power, skills, strength, and stamina to face each new challenge squarely, and with an attitude that failure isn't an option.

If you have a heavy heart—whether it's in relation to a partner, friend, job, or lifestyle—and it grows into a nagging sense that won't go away, then I believe that's your gut guiding you. I am convinced that my gut tells me the truth. I have learned to have faith in myself and not shy away from what my intuition is telling me; it may be ugly and raw, but it is honest. Little did I know that my intentions of setting aside time to attend class parties and go on field trips would later allow me to redirect my time to devote to my son whose mental health challenges would slowly start to surface. My time and focus now pivoted from participating in PTO to talking with school administrators, going to doctor appointments, researching new resources and medications, investigating alternative learning opportunities, and more.

Let's be honest, all of us have a friend, family member, colleague, or acquaintance who struggles with mental health challenges. Then throw in the invention of the cell phone and social media and many parents may think all hope is lost. When I was a kid, life was simple. I would call my dad to pick me up at the mall by using a quarter at a payphone. In addition, when I was a teen, mental wellness simply wasn't talked about. If I showed that my family was suffering, it was interpreted as inadequacy or a character flaw. My family quietly suffered through suicide, depression, bipolar swings, and more. Understanding my genetics and what I may have passed down to my son drove me to speak up for him because he simply didn't have a voice and could not advocate for himself.

Jake was in fourth grade when his father and I realized that he was continuing to get into trouble at school, arguing with staff and students. He was losing friends and falling academically behind. It was at this time that reality hit all of us, and with vengeance. We could see his increased anxiety and sadness, along with a lack of focus. It took us years to fully understand what our son has been saddled with and the burden he carried. After a heated debate with another parent, I wanted to dig in and learn about mental health and how I could help support Jake's ever-changing world.

During my interviews with mental health professionals, there was one comment I heard that was profound. This therapist told me mental health is a struggle for outside people to understand, especially if that child appears to be "normal." If my son had looked physically different, then his challenges would be obvious. With mental health, people cannot see the issue and it becomes much harder for them to process and ultimately sympathize with Jake's situation. This excellent insight is one I continue to reflect on, because soon afterward we were chasing a myriad of medical ghosts: symptoms, medications, and therapies. It became even more clear that both listening to myself (gut) and persevering would change Jake's life for the better.

Any family member who has firsthand experience with "extreme parenting" knows the gut-wrenching days and nights. One of my best resources was enlisting a child advocate to help us navigate the educational system with resources outside the school day. We were fortunate to afford an experienced advocate who made a profound and positive difference, but parents can also turn to organizations that offer child advocating services and support with little or no out-of-pocket costs. Parents must commit the time, but the resources we need are out there and ready to find. It took us three psychiatrists and numerous therapists to find "the one," and that result is imperative. Even if it takes cycling through a few professionals, it's crucial to find one that fits the child, their needs, and what is comfortable for the whole family. I also learned that enlisting a patient advocate with our health insurance company was an option that saved hours of frustration and arguments.

During our family's journey, we learned that mainstream public school wasn't the right fit for our son. He needed an alternative resource. I'm not speaking negatively about public school; but it did come down to what would best help Jake become academically successful. For some families this may mean homeschooling or attending a smaller school with more or less structure, but no one knows a child better than the parents; they know what environment their child will thrive in.

No parent should be afraid to speak up and ask for help. I am reminded each day that it is OK to ask for help, and I'm amazed at what can result from a conversation with a stranger when I simply share my story. Nearly everyone I speak with has a similar story or knows of someone who is dealing with the same things that I am! Camaraderie is an empowering feeling.

It's been a few years since my first Aha! Moment, and I'm still growing and learning how to best support my son. But I've also opened my world and heart to alternative methods of treatment that I wouldn't have even considered a year ago. And so, the journey with my son, business, and life continues. With every dark day there are two brighter days that follow, bringing comfort and hope. Those on a similar path may be reassured that there is light at the end of the tunnel. However, there is no end game when treating mental health; it's a rotating door. But as a gentle reminder, we can fall back on others during our most challenging moments and remind ourselves that we and our families are worthy and loved…and it's OK to ask for help along the way.

RESOURCES

Child Advocacy Support https://bit.ly/43j0Yek

Rx 101: Making Mental Health Medications Easy(er) to Understand https://bit.ly/46GOkIW

Behavioral Health Response Support https://bit.ly/3rqz1nS

Finding the Right Mental Health Care Insurance https://bit.ly/3pINqv0

Behavioral Health Nutrition https://bit.ly/3JSYahk

Parent Self-Care https://bit.ly/3pFkFiI

Laura DeVries owns CommCore Marketing, a certified Woman-Owned Business Enterprise based in St. Charles, Missouri, founded in 2014. Laura has more than twenty-five years of marketing and communications experience, managing a variety of business-to-business and business-to-consumer accounts, including nonprofits, manufacturing, SaaS, and a Fortune 500 company. Laura excels at increasing sales and brand awareness, as well as creating successful marketing campaigns and building a strong online presence for clients. She is passionate about supporting the community and giving back through volunteering. Laura serves on the board of directors for several organizations. Her mental health advocacy began shortly after the inception of her company and continues to grow, as she faces ongoing challenges and hurdles associated with supporting the health and well-being of her son, Jacob.

Lynn Baribault

Am I Really Enough as I Am Now?

Life is made of extraordinary choices. At twenty-seven, I moved to Southeast Asia to teach and head the United Nations Volunteers' office in a small country. There, I married and had two beautiful daughters. As a result of traumatic circumstances, I felt forced to take my daughters and flee. For four months, we could not safely leave without raising too much suspicion…it felt so long. Finally, all was in place to allow me to leave with both daughters, not just one.

Friends drove us across the border, where we missed our first flight. We hired a taxi to drive us through the night, enabling us to board our connecting flight to Canada. As we went through Customs, my daughters and I were stopped and escorted to an airport security room. I was inwardly frantic, wondering what would happen to us.

I thought my ex had flagged us and that we would be caught. Both daughters were asleep, one in my arms and the other in her stroller. Just before the security guards started asking questions, my eldest daughter woke up and started chatting with me, quickly confirming my role as her mother. Thankfully, they let us go. I was relieved, realizing that the officers had thought I, a Caucasian woman, was illegally taking Asian-looking children out of the country. We made it safely to Canada.

We fled our home with one backpack each, filled with food, clothes, books, and games. To this day, I still have no idea how we made this journey.

Once in Canada, I was on welfare for a year and then resumed teaching. We did not have much, but we had each other. I raised myself out of poverty and have had a beautiful life. I know Spirit protected me; they understood more than I acknowledged: that I was worthy of so much more than just my traumatic experiences.

"I am enough!" I say with gusto! Hmmm…not quite right, so I try again: "I. Am. Enough," trying to speak each word firmly. Still not quite there. So I try once more. "I am…enough?" And end with a big question mark. Then, of course, I just feel defeated.

Over the course of my life, I have often felt inspired—on top of the world, even—but then quickly fallen back down, thinking that my skills, choices, hopes, and dreams didn't amount to much.

I know I am kind. I know I have heart. I know I am an independent, caring, and intelligent woman. I also know that, as many of you reading this, I have surmounted incredible difficulties, trauma, and hardships. Not only do I fail to give myself credit for my gifts, my joy, and my blessings, I even view my life's challenges as "not as hard" as what others have gone through. From whichever scale I judge myself, I have often felt I was never enough. This skewed perspective leaves me unable to fully heal.

I am unsure why this is my "go-to" pattern. I have worked hard all my life to decipher the depth of my heart, to clearly see my patterns, and to "unlearn" the "realities" I have chosen to believe.

Today, the "I am enough" statements bombarding us from all directions have the opposite of the desired effect on me. Viewing the social media fantasies many people post about their magical lives, I end up feeling inadequate, as I instinctively compare myself to their perceived successes. While still celebrating others' beautiful moments and their ways of marking important occasions, I ponder whether their images create an illusion, or that perhaps they, like me, are trying to convince themselves that we all possess a great magical life.

When will it be my turn to truly feel that I am enough? I sincerely don't know, and, honestly, these inner musings leave me depleted, defeated, and deflated. If you are like me, you remain mostly positive and try again. Maybe that is because, in our deepest inner selves and through our inner knowing, we acknowledge that our uniqueness is simply that: unique.

All of us being humans, our go-to is to compare ourselves to others, as they are our barometer for gauging our own success, happiness, wealth, and life. Why do we keep doing this? Why do we beat ourselves down, making comparisons to other humans who are not us, who don't have the same set of skills and attributes our DNA carries? Isn't our own brand of uniqueness enough? Why do we feel the need to continuously measure up to others who are not us and will never be us?

When taking the time to get past my annoyance, jealousy, and envy at watching others' lives through their rose-colored lenses, I start to acknowledge my feelings. As I analyze my life, successes, traumas, and challenges, I grow stronger, wiser, and develop a greater understanding of my own heart. When I stop comparing, I find a long list of ways that I am good…and maybe good enough!

Because of my life, who I am, and what I have learned, I am a better listener. I have learned to listen from my heart and hear more of what's behind one's words to get to the true meaning of the issues being shared. I also have much empathy for others as they themselves go through their own mix of the great, the good, the bad, and the worse.

I notice that people, whether known to me or random strangers, easily share their stories with me. It amazes me that people feel comfortable and willing to share in this way. My gift then is to listen, say a few encouraging words, and smile as I leave, or continue to pay attention, simply being fully there for friends and family.

When I reflect further on this way of being present, I know in my heart that I am enough for that person at that moment. It feels wonderful and warms my heart. I know who I am. I know what I, as an individual, bring to the table. I know I am proud of where I am in my own life and what I have learned, so shouldn't that mean that I am indeed enough as I am?

When comparing ourselves to others, it's as if we are comparing oranges to bananas. In this metaphor, we are all fruit, yet we are each our own type of fruit; we are each unique. We need to start acknowledging ourselves with and within our own stories. When I reflect upon the statement "I am enough" and simply look at myself and my life, without reference to others, I feel more ready to say that, indeed, I am enough.

Yet I sometimes like to qualify such statements to make them feel more attainable. I would prefer to say "I am enough *at the moment*" or "I am content with being enough *for now*" or "Being enough for oneself is a journey in itself."

This process of moving into my own discomfort and beyond the complex meanderings of my mind always adjusts my perceptions and beliefs. Now I realize that my mind is but one small part of who I am. Each of us can come to know that our uniqueness comprises many intrinsic parts, including our heart, our Soul, our connections to Spirit, the Divine, Mother Earth, and to the people in our lives who truly love us for who we are, faults and all.

In the full complexity of being ourselves, we can only compare our growth, heart, gifts, and joys to the person we were in our youth…or even last year. Who we are now in adulthood is only fully seen through the depth of our learning, in our heart, and in the incredible resilience of our own Spirit.

When I honestly connect to these deep places, I know I am whole. I know I am heart. I know I am. And, in this beautiful moment of realization, with gentleness and acceptance for my journey, I can finally say that, indeed, I am enough.

Care to join me? Here is a simple exercise to expand your sense of being enough. In the morning, as you may already do, write a list of tasks or goals you truly want to achieve that day—but keep it to just three realistic items. Next, write two actions that bring you joy. Simple things like watching your puppy play or your baby sleep are fine! Lastly, as we all have larger dreams we wish to see come true, add one item that is a step toward one of your important aspirations. It may be for a dream you hide even from yourself, believing you will never have the time or the resources to achieve it. Now, post these five items on your Own My Joy list where you can see it all day, and get started on them! Check off those tasks, yes…and also get some joy in your day and take a step toward your dreams.

Each item, regardless of which list it came from, is a gift to yourself. Yes, even washing the floors can be joyful and joy filled if you make it a conscious choice. Infuse each to-do with love and happiness, celebrating yourself when you are done or when you have taken a few steps toward completion. Acknowledge each as a success in your day. Cross them off and start again the next day. Now, as we all know, some goals and dreams will take longer to realize, or they may transform with time, but that shouldn't stop you from celebrating each step along the way.

By doing this simple exercise of reframing your to-do lists, and by adding deeper purpose to each item, you will start to feel more accomplished and happier with yourself. These feelings, in turn, will encourage you to continue to step forward, and very soon you will find that completing even menial tasks brings you closer to realizing your larger dreams.

Life is a series of moments, so why not aim for beauty, satisfaction, and progress? Who doesn't like to celebrate and be celebrated?

You are totally worth it, and so am I!

Lynn Baribault is an intuitive channeler, author, and a certified practitioner for The Compassion Key®. She offers insightful, channelled guidance, oracle card readings, Ohana Generational Healing sessions, and teaches intuition and channelling classes. Lynn is a retired elementary school teacher and an end-of-life doula. Lynn's first vision came when she was only six years old. Since then, she has developed her intuition and connection to Spirit. Being able to hear, feel, and see Spirit, she offers insights for the peace of mind, heart, and soul. Lynn feels truly blessed to have been gifted so many skills, which she is thrilled to share with her clients, family, and friends. Lynn is the proud author of *How to Raise Your Children with Wisdom and Awareness* and is currently working on other books. She enjoys the opportunity to grow, learn, trust, and share the wisdom of the spirit world! Her life motto is "Peace within is peace living."

Megan Rieke

And Then There Was Joy

My mother tells me I was a happy baby—all eyes and a big gummy smile. Even as an awkward teenager, with headgear and a mouth full of metal, I was foolishly and simply happy. I endured significant trauma and grief during childhood, which chipped away at my inherent joy. As an eighteen-year-old, I had lost myself before I had begun to be myself.

But I'm stubborn and refused to let anyone or any situation rule me. I went to college. I went to therapy. I volunteered. I traveled. I became that happy girl again. I emerged. I realized the real journey in life is to simply live as myself because that's the road to pure joy.

I approached getting pregnant at twenty-three with the same zest that I approached all my adventures. I wasn't scared, but my boyfriend was. Instructed by his father to marry me, he proposed, and I said yes. I didn't plan for my life to take this route, and I was elated for the beautiful adventures ahead for my little family. My fiancé and I would do things better than our parents. We would show our baby boy that a loving couple is composed of two people who create a partnership through healthy communication, respect, love, and emotional maturity.

That didn't turn out to be the case.

The first time I died inside was when our baby was six weeks old. He cried constantly. I wasn't allowed to give him a pacifier. Even though he had already nursed and I had no more milk, we would lie together with my flaccid breast in his mouth to pacify him. I held him against my chest all day and night, trying to create an external womb for him. Although it was hard and I cried from exhaustion often, I loved him in a way I had never known love.

His pediatrician told me he had colic. When my husband came home from work, I was cradling our son, who was suckling my milk-less breasts. "Good news!" I exclaimed. "The reason he cries all of the time is because he has colic! Nobody really knows what it is, but he's gaining weight and everything is OK! We just have to wait for him to outgrow it!" My husband, expressionless, looked at our son, then looked at me. "No son of mine is weak or sick. He doesn't have colic. You just can't handle being a mother." I put my head down in shame and agreed.

Mother. Mom. Mama. What a feeling of honor those names gave me. But his words immediately stripped away any sense of doing *anything* right for my baby. The moment I accepted the lie that I was a Bad Mom was the moment I became afraid to be *Mom* at all.

I lowered my head in shame and agreement.

I met my husband after I graduated college while working on a small cruise ship. Poetry, romanticism, and idealism blinded me from reality. I had seen our chance meeting as fate. What I thought was love was simply his turn to "hit on" the new girl—me. What I first framed as "trying harder to make everything work out" turned out to be me saying yes when I wanted to say no. Each day was a cut to my soul that no one saw, including myself.

Adding two more boys to our little brood piled more stress on him and more responsibilities on me as stay-at-home mom, maid, chauffeur, accountant, landscaper, laundress, go-fer, and chef. The more hats I wore, the more I craved his ever-elusive approval. The more I asked for it, the more he told me why I didn't deserve it. I accepted his judgment as fact. The twenty-one-year-old, happy, naïve girl he had met many moons ago was officially dead.

I lived in a perpetual state of fear throughout my marriage: When will he scream at me in public? When will he ignore me for days? Tell the boys it's my job to clean, not theirs? When will he sit impatiently in the car for forty-five minutes while I gather side dishes, kids, and their gear for a family barbeque?

When will he tell me what I think and feel? Mock me for not having a paying job but threaten to divorce me if I get one? When will he belittle my art career? Yell at me to stop crying over my dead dad? Call me a f^@%ing bitch after I've given birth the second time? When will he tell me my friends are using me?

When will he come home, eat family dinner in ten minutes, then leave the kids and me sitting alone and stupefied? When will he watch me mow grass, weed, dig holes, repair, paint, replace, haul, and heave, then tell me it's my choice so he doesn't need to help? When will he laugh at my lingerie and tell me I'm not sexy? Brush off my snuggles and tell me I'm needy? Tell me that he doesn't have to hug me today because he spent enough time hugging me in 2003?

When will he tell my mother I'm broken and it's her fault? Declare my college degree is stupid? Tell our oldest that I'm sick and he needs to protect his brothers from me? When will he scream at our middle that he's sick like me? Tell me I'm a failure and can't make it without him? When will he announce that he doesn't love me and didn't love me even when we got married?

The first time I sliced myself was the first time I felt peace in over a decade. I had grown accustomed to bashing my temples with knuckled fists, but that insult only gave me lumps. I tried bashing my skull against walls, but that only caused ringing in my ears. After yet another incident hearing how terrible I was, I sat in the kitchen alone. I refused to cry anymore. My insides were seething like my guts had become gnarled teeth. With a clenched jaw and clenched fist, I picked up a butcher knife, knowing the blade was thick and couldn't cause any real damage. I swiftly dug it into my forearm. There was blood. I watched it ooze as I felt those gnarled teeth inside of me retract. My jaw and fists softened. I breathed deeply, refreshed like a clean pair of underwear.

As the abuse and toxicity escalated over more years, so did my resolve to find peace through dripping blood. I eventually graduated to razors and wrists. I was not suicidal, but I no longer believed in my right to take up space. I didn't want to die, but I didn't want to live. Years of his criticism taught me I was a waste of skin, so why did it matter if I shredded mine? It was one of the few things I could call my own, after all. Tired of trying to convince him I was neither sick nor bad, I became the sickest and the "baddest" version of myself so he would stop.

I screamed. I threw s%!t. I hit. I damaged my kids. I slept with another man. I was admitted twice for inpatient treatment. I lashed out at everyone. I decided I was God's s%!t bag. I drank too much. I denounced happiness. I accepted an existence of mediocrity. I gave up.

Why did I feel safer in a pool of my own blood than in my own kitchen?

What makes emotional abuse so painful is how you start to mistrust yourself. I became animalistic, ruled by my amygdala, my primitive brain. My humanity crumbled beneath the priority to survive as I quietly sat, anticipating the next attack. My joy, my smile, my laugh, anything that made me *me* was stripped away. The only thing stronger than my own survival was my mama-bear instinct. Protecting my kids was the reason I emotionally limped through life.

So I kept disobeying their father. I maintained friendships and created art. I desperately sought to hold onto a semblance of my own happiness so my kids could keep theirs pure. The more I defied him, the angrier he became. The more we fought, the more I cut. The sicker I became, the more righteous he appeared.

But then I decided to start trying again. I remembered how I had been lost before and how I had found myself. Despite veering away from all of my core values within every role I played, I mustered up the courage to look in the mirror. Day by day, I would tell myself, even though I didn't believe it, that I wasn't a bad mom or sick. Despite becoming a girl wholly unrecognizable to myself, I knew there was a nugget of my mother's bald-headed daughter curled up somewhere deep in my soul, grinning wildly.

I went into the woods and found that girl, the one I used to be, buried beneath trauma, shame, guilt, and best intentions. I lifted her out of the pile of leaves and brought her into the sunshine. She looked different than I had expected. She was sweet, tender, soft, scared, and vulnerable. I began to familiarize myself with her and grew to love her. I gratefully became her and began another adventure to find a different kind of joy within myself.

Megan Rieke is a mom, artist, and writer living in St. Louis, Missouri. Her paintings hang in private collections around the country, and her work has been featured in *Forbes* and *Midwest Living*, among other local publications. As a recent grant recipient from the Regional Arts Commission, she will produce another solo exhibit in 2024. When she's not making dad jokes and correcting her sons' grammar, she spends time with her partner in Kentucky rehabbing an old house.

Nancy Thompson

Borrowed Confidence

The white envelope could've gotten lost in the pile of mail on my desk. Except this one was different. It was addressed to *me*—at work! All the others were addressed to management, for me to open and sort or "handle." Maybe one of my coworkers entered my name in a crazy contest and this was just the junk mail that action generated. *Oh well*, I thought. *I'll probably just get a laugh out of it and pitch it in the trash can.*

Nope—not junk mail. This piece of mail was serious. The mortgage company needed answers, and they needed them now. The words on the page seemed to jump out and hit me right between the eyes! One question had me particularly nervous: "Probability of continued employment?" How could I even answer that question? What *was* the right answer?

What was I supposed to do now? Single and barely twenty-three years old, I had just signed a contract on my first house, which prompted papers from the mortgage company to begin the loan process. This paperwork landed on my desk the same day a company-wide announcement was made that my employer of four years was relocating to another state. That meant about 90 percent of all employees would be laid off—including me.

Proceeding with my plan to buy a house seemed out of the question given this shocking news. After months of searching for just the right one, I was just days away from my goal of home ownership, and I now knew I was going to have to postpone my dream. What a disappointment. If the mortgage company only knew what had just transpired in my world, the form would not have been mailed at all and my dream would've died right then and there.

Receiving the news of losing my job at the same time I was applying for a mortgage felt disconcerting. It seemed to create a perfect storm that I quickly saw only as potential obstacles to achieving my goals. I say potential because they really were just bumps in the road that I needed to get around.

What was I to do now? As I sought answers from coworkers—those I considered older and wiser—I saw a variety of emotions. Some were bitter, some worried, some confused … and all were shocked. It was the 1980s, corporate reorganizations were rampant, and this was my first layoff. To add to this sudden and new uncertainty about my future, management wasn't sure when our last day of employment would be. It was an opportunity for me to uplevel my self-confidence and test my risk tolerance. I was a risk taker; however, I was no gambler.

This day had started out like any other day. I wiped the sleep out of my eyes, put my hair up in my timer-preheated hot rollers, and got dressed for work. I still had some prep work to complete for the two college classes I would rush to right after work that night. Little did I know that the day would have several unexpected surprises, which would cause me to think quickly on my feet. In fact, this day would require me to repeatedly attempt to regain whatever sense of control I thought I had over my life.

I had really enjoyed the job, the company, and the people I worked with, so this news meant more than a financial loss for me.

By day I worked in an office full time, and at night I went to school full time. I had no other source of income and no one else to provide financially, should I be unable to afford my proposed new house payment.

There was no Plan B, and I was hoping to move into that house the following month. Yikes—time was short!

How was I supposed to find another job so quickly and stay on schedule with school and my home purchase? I had the timing all worked out... or so I thought. It was important for me to stay on the job until the undetermined end date, to collect the bonus offered for those who did so as that bonus was now earmarked for house payments.

And what about college? Did this job loss mean I was going to lose my ability to buy a house *and* also to finish college? Finishing college meant going on to do even bigger and better things in my work life. I was meant for more than being a secretary, and I knew that within my core. I had more in me. I wasn't sure what my destiny was to be, but I did know this job was a stepping stone, rather than a final destination.

I was working full time to pay for college, and my employer was supplementing that investment. Working full time and going to night school meant I had little time for homework. I had been using lunch hours, staying late after work, or going in on weekends to type papers and do homework. How could I fit a job search into that schedule?

The benefit of tuition assistance was one of the reasons I chose to work for that company. Could I find another job that would also have a college tuition program, so I could complete my education? Tuition reimbursement was uncommon in corporate America at the time, and it was a very nice supplement to my income. How could I afford to finish school without it?

These thoughts all raced through my mind as I stared at the words on that innocent mortgage checklist. Although I was a fairly confident person at that young age, this had me shaken.

This time-sensitive paperwork had to be completed *now* to fulfill my dream of purchasing a house—a goal I'd set at age seventeen. Purchasing this house was to be the largest accomplishment I would achieve in my young life thus far. *What mortgage company would lend money to a kid with no job?* I thought. *What should I do?*

To overcome my lack of confidence at that moment, I had to focus on my goals rather than my insecurities. I needed something or someone to put things in perspective and boost my confidence.

I called my real estate agent to fill her in. She knew me well enough to know that the probability of continued employment was certain. She told me to answer the question about the likelihood of continued employment with one word—Excellent! As she said it, I actually believed it! She had so much confidence in me that I realized *yes, she is right!* I have skills and am resourceful. I *will* get another job, and I *will* purchase this house and close on schedule.

I also looked at the most extreme, worst-case scenario. What if I couldn't afford the house payment? The answer was simple—I'd get sent to jail, where they'd provide me with food, clothing, and a roof over my head. Not ideal, but that would meet my basic needs, right?

So it was settled; I was moving forward. And if I needed help with finances, I would get a roommate to share the costs. I do realize that the reality was if I couldn't make my house payment, the house would be repossessed by the mortgage company. However, like I said, I was considering the worst case.

The paperwork went through seamlessly, and I got the loan. I was even able to take advantage of a first-time homeowner's interest rate, which, at just over 13 percent, was better than any of the rates at the time. My work with that fabulous company ended a couple of months later, and I stayed until they closed the doors. I received my additional bonus, and I had a plan.

Money was a concern. However, I had excellent skills and knew I could work for a temporary agency and support myself while I pursued my next permanent job.

Since I possessed terrific office skills in the latest technology, I knew I could nail the interview and skills testing to get started on a work assignment within the same week.

And that's what I did. I became employed as a temporary office worker, choosing the best-known agency to apply to first.

My experience as a temp allowed me exposure to several top companies, and that's how I secured my next permanent job. And the new company also provided tuition reimbursement. Free from interruptions in my college education, that new employer also paid for most of my undergraduate education and two graduate degrees.

Added benefits were that my take-home pay was even higher than at my former job and I was exposed to a variety of new opportunities and on-the-job education.

Fortunately, the former homeowners needed to stay in "my" house for an additional couple of months. This godsend helped me out, too, because the rent they paid me exceeded the mortgage payments.

With the confidence the real estate agent exhibited in me, she revealed that my drive and motivation were attributes she saw better than I did. In effect, I borrowed her confidence in me until I could own it. That's how the concept of Borrowed Confidence was born. Who can lend you some confidence to help you on your journey? And who do you know who might benefit from a loan you can offer?

During more than thirty years in a multi-million-dollar annual sales geography, Nancy Thompson worked for several Fortune 100 and 500 companies. Her work in sales and marketing management, client relationship management, and consultative/solution selling earned multiple national sales trips, awards, and contests. Nancy is a graduate of multiple professional sales trainings and has, in turn, trained hundreds of sales leaders, incorporating neuroscience to close the gap between internal thinking and external sales results. Nancy was integral to the launch of five successful corporate and commercial sales organizations, from positions of sales manager, sales trainer, director of sales, and director of marketing. She holds two master's degrees—in Marketing and Computer Information Management—as well as her BA in Business Administration/Management. Nancy's other certifications include: Master Coach and Trainer in Neuro-Linguistic Programming (NLP), and Master Practitioner of Integrated Time Line. She is also a graduate of Success Mastery I and II, and a certified confidence coach.

Natalie Taylor-Levin

The Best Is Yet to Come

When I was eleven years old, I woke in the night to see the silhouette of a man in the doorway of my bedroom. As he approached my bedside, I noticed he was naked, and my mind became clouded with confusion, uncertainty, and fear. Frozen in place, unable to move, I longed to become invisible, a tiny speck. In an instant, I was trapped, held in place by what felt like a giant boulder. The assault that ensued that night was a complete betrayal of my trust by someone I knew and loved. It left me traumatized, and that trauma remained with me for years.

I'm finally sharing this story from my childhood, which has needed to be told for more than four decades. After avoiding and stuffing those memories down for so long, I'm ready to move forward free of the guilt and shame I've carried my whole life. This shame was never mine to carry.

The truth is, there's no one roadmap to navigate sexual assault, so we just put one foot in front of the other, sometimes stumbling around, in hopes that we'll figure it out as we go along. Fortunately, I was able to find my way to true healing, and the road I took to get there was off the beaten path.

When I moved into my first apartment years ago, I became free to live life on my own terms. I decided that no one was going to make me do anything without my consent, ever again. I just wanted to live life to the fullest, and to never allow my past to hinder me from whatever I wanted to achieve or do in life. For the most part, I've been successful, but my internal struggle still got in the way even when I did my best to avoid it. The problem is, when you live your life in spite of something, you're still attached to it.

Because of my past, I was interested in learning about human behavior and understanding why we do what we do. I read anything I could get my hands on to expand my knowledge about self-care, persevering, and personal growth. I also found the sport of running and began participating in organized running races in the early 1990s. Running gave me the opportunity to push through physical pain, which felt like a healing release to me, grinding it out with every footstep. Mile after mile, as I got into the flow, I could sort out my thoughts, gain clarity, and enjoy some moments of freedom from the internal struggle. Running was my drug of choice. It was my freedom.

Over the years, I've tried on a lot of strategies for overcoming the past, but the deep inner healing still went virtually untouched. Then a fortunate thing happened. I came across a simple Pause practice that was the turning point in my healing journey. The Pause helped me calm my mind when my thoughts were sporadic, critical, or negative, and when I felt annoyed, anxious, or upset. Over time, using this practice, I broke an internal pattern of worry and fear. Pausing was like pressing a reset button.

Pausing gave my mind a moment of rest and helped put things into perspective. When annoyed or upset, I began choosing a more helpful response over a knee-jerk reaction. I no longer felt compelled to spend so much of my precious time and energy taking things personally, judging myself, and getting caught up in petty things.

Continuing the Pause, I began experiencing more moments of true peace, clarity, and creativity. I began journaling about my life and childhood. Writing has helped me remember the many loving people and experiences I had in my life when I was growing up. It has helped me see clearly how I'd allowed one incident to overshadow so many beautiful moments. Once I was able to get the story out of me and onto paper, I began to feel more alive, more in charge of my life and emotions, and I began to find my voice.

Then, truly open to healing and doing the work, a recovery journey began to unfold before me and within me. It was like the universe said, "OK now you're ready; here are the tools you need." I watched a documentary that shared a healing exercise where you visualize a time when you felt inferior, despondent, embarrassed, rejected, and/or ashamed, and you ask your shadow (your past), "How do you feel about how I've treated you?" and "What can I do to make it up to you?"

Immediately, answers came to mind. My younger self felt like I had denied her voice, her feelings, her needs, and her dreams. And, to make it up to her, I needed to be brave and tell the story. After doing this exercise, I felt an immense pull to dig more deeply into the idea that I had let my inner child down. I decided to sit in quiet, visualizing myself entering my childhood home.

In my visioning, I ventured up the stairs to my old bedroom and found my younger self sitting on the edge of her bed, wearing pajamas, her head facing down. I could hear her quietly crying. In that moment, I felt my heart expand with so much love for her. I walked over to her. I sat down beside her on the bed. I reached out to her and gently pulled her close to me. I held her in my arms, rocking her, cradling her with so much love and letting her cry until her tears dried up. The love I felt for this sweet, hurting child was more love than I'd ever experienced.

Healing continued as I repeated this process of visioning, again and again. Over many visits to my younger self, I continued to console her, simply sitting and being present with her, loving on her. I started to find this exercise was bringing me much comfort and healing. I wanted to spend time with her, wanted her to feel better, wanted to make sure she truly understood just how loved she was and that she was safe.

Visiting my past, at a time when I was at my lowest point, reentering over and over the room and the moment I'd avoided my whole life, was akin to putting together a thousand-piece jigsaw puzzle, having only the outer edges done. Each time I sat in quiet connection to my past, I was able to put one more puzzle piece into the inner parts of the experience. Soon my image was almost complete, and I was becoming whole again.

Then, one morning I got up early for a run. As I settled into my normal pace, I felt the desire to go through this healing exercise while in motion. I began to slowly go through the familiar process: visualizing myself walking up the stairs of my childhood home and making my way toward my old bedroom. As I stood in the doorway, I could see my younger self sitting on the edge of the bed, wearing the same nightgown, with her head facing down as usual.

As I took a step toward her, she looked up at me and took my breath away. She had a wide, bright smile on her face. It was like she was excited to see me and had been expecting me, waiting for me. She stood up, reached for my hands, and we clasped our hands tightly together. We felt so much love and happiness in that moment that we began swirling around in circles, laughing, and jumping for joy together until we were dizzy. When we stopped, we stood face-to-face and looked deeply into each other's eyes. Without words, I knew she was ready to leave this place. Together we turned, hand-in-hand, and left my childhood home forever.

I can no longer go to the past to sit and visit with my inner child because she doesn't live there anymore. Now, I simply pause, place my hand on my chest, breathe, and feel her within me. I look directly into my eyes in the mirror, and I see her there, looking back at me. I tell her how much I love her, and how much she means to me. I remind her she is safe, healed, and whole. Together, we are certain that the best is yet to come.

Natalie Taylor-Levin is a writer, athlete, and registered dietitian with a focus on whole foods and functional nutrition. She is the owner of Moxie Health and Wellness Solutions where she partners with clients to help them heal their relationship with food and reach their health and wellness goals. She loves gardening, outdoor patios, gelato, warm weather, and spending quality time with her husband, Steven, and their dog, Remy.

Pamela Fenili

Cracks in the Crystal Ball

When we arrive in life, we each start as a perfectly smooth, shiny crystal ball. Experiences, people we encounter, and things we absorb over time can chip away at that pure surface and eventually form cracks: some hairline, some that cut deep. These cracks cause alarm at first, but as we age we may realize these cracks are the key to our awakening.

The first crack in my crystal appeared at age eight. My forty-six-year-old dad, my rock, my biggest fan, left for work and never returned. A highway patrol officer found him slumped over the steering wheel, dead on the side of the freeway.

I'll never forget that night. I knew something was wrong when he wasn't home for dinner. Our house was silent. My mom sat in the darkness in the living room, staring out the front window, waiting for him to drive up, for hours. She sent me to bed around nine p.m., but there was *no way* I was going to sleep without kissing my dad good night!

Around nine thirty, I heard a car pull up! I ran to a window facing the street and ripped open the curtains. It was a highway patrol car, and I watched my mom walk toward the officer. They spoke and then Mom fell to her knees, screaming. In my young mind, I formed the idea that my dad had been hurt in a car accident. Then, my mom sent me across the street to the neighbors, with no explanation. I was really confused, as it was late.

The first crack in my crystal started to form, and it was significant. I grew more and more uncomfortable by the minute, sitting in my neighbor's kitchen as multiple cars arrived at my house. Whenever I heard a car, I ran to the window thinking it was my dad…but it wasn't. When my grandparents' car pulled up at almost midnight, arriving from their home more than an hour away, I realized the truth might be worse than I had imagined. The crack grew bigger.

When my neighbor went to the bathroom, I bolted back across the street and burst through the front door of my house. It was packed with relatives, family friends, and my older siblings; everyone had been crying. I found Mom sitting in the kitchen and asked her why we weren't on our way to the hospital to see my dad. What she said next stopped time.

All the sound around me ceased. Movement slid eerily into slow motion. She explained he wasn't in the hospital and that we wouldn't be going to visit him because he died—he was *never* coming home again. Ever.

In the silence of shock, I ran and locked myself in the bathroom. *Why was she lying to me? How could she say something so horrible??* My parents often had verbal arguments in front of me, so it wasn't far-fetched that my mom would say something crazy (it wouldn't be the first time). I was struggling to rationalize everything as any child that age would. The crack was so *deep* now, it almost cut me into pieces. Over the next several days, I realized my mom wasn't lying. He was never coming home. *Ever.*

This first crack in my crystal ball opened the way for more to come. My perfect, shiny crystal exterior had been weakened, and I had no idea how vulnerable that would make me for years ahead. You see, my mom taught me to "keep busy" and keep moving, because she always said that my pain, grief, and wounded heart would all resolve over time.

A year later, I was struggling with a brokenness everyone else could see, while my mom entirely focused on fixing the cracks in her own crystal. She was rarely home and had started dating. She even moved out of our house and into her boyfriend's, leaving me alone for almost two years. Yes, at nine years of age. My sisters, older by five and eight years, helped me as they could around their jobs and social lives, but I spent *a lot* of time alone. Sometimes bills went unpaid and we had no electricity or running water. We had very little food at home, sometimes none! I never knew where my next meal would come from, but I always managed to scrounge enough bus money to get back and forth to school every day. School and sports were my escape, my normalcy.

My private school provided weekly counseling with a therapist. During one session, the counselor realized that I was living alone, and that day I got off the bus to find a police officer and another person chatting with my mom on our front porch. Immediately after that, she moved back in and brought her boyfriend with her.

After that, I spent the next handful of my tween and early teenage years doing anything and everything to escape the house. Searching to repair some of my cracks, I made so many more! I'm surprised I didn't bust my crystal ball entirely because I was searching in *all the wrong places*! I had my first drink at eleven. By sixteen, I was utterly lost, with alcohol and recreational drugs as a way of life. No structure, rules, or curfews. I moved from day to day with no direction, purpose, or self-worth. With nobody at home knowing or caring where I was going, I could do whatever I wanted. And after all the food insecurity of those two years alone, I also developed a significant eating disorder. Then I met my soon-to-be husband, and he had lots of cracks too! Perfect match! At first we filled some of the other's voids, and he provided a safe space. Determined to heal these deep cracks in our crystals, we moved in together at seventeen and married at twenty-one.

For the first time, I felt whole. Solid. A year later, we brought a shiny, new, perfectly beautiful crystal ball into this world: our daughter Sydney.

Looking at her, I knew I needed to change. To keep her safe, to protect her from cracks in her innocent life. The intention was real, but the know-how was not, after stuffing years of pain and grief. Five years later another perfect crystal ball rolled into this world: our daughter Camryn. Now I had responsibility for two perfect people who we were blessed with creating. Two shiny, perfect, precious, and innocent crystal balls as a source of healing our own cracks and for a do-over of my mom's mistakes.

Over the next decade, my cracks spread and deepened. Years of neglecting my feelings were catching up with me. Food and alcohol allowed me to cope and escape, and seemed natural in our society that focuses on celebrating and socializing. We seemed a perfect family, but I was still cracked and broken.

The pain and grief that often leaked through my cracks made life harder for others, and sometimes unbearable for me. So I ran, just as my mom did, just as other family members had done. Striving to prevent any cracks in my beautiful family, I gave them one of the most significant of their lives. The divorce cracked us all.

I ran away fast and hard…and fell right on my face, almost losing everything. But here is where the healing started: when the cracks stopped forming and spreading. This is when I realized I had a choice and began to feel hope. Sitting on the ground at rock bottom, looking up, I saw options not visible before. In fact, I saw my life as a series of choices, and how every choice made me. I had been allowing life to happen *to me* instead of making choices *for me*.

The first choice in a new direction was to reclaim my health, the biggest hurdle because I'd been layering on unhealthy habits for decades.

On my forty-fifth birthday, I chose. Each day of nine months, I chose me, and I never looked back. I lost one hundred and eight pounds that had taken decades to pile on, released in about two hundred and seventy days. Removing layers and layers of physical weight also peeled away self-doubt and shame, filling so many of the cracks with something other than the weight. My crystal ball was starting to shine again!

Happy for the first time since early childhood, I had energy, hope, and drive! I couldn't know that another crystal-cracking event was coming. My beautiful sister, Pia—also my ride-or-die best friend—was diagnosed with a very aggressive form of breast cancer, and the illness came on fast and hard. Raising money, fighting hurdles in the healthcare system, we got her into a cancer treatment facility, but it was too late. I sat with her, cared for her, carried her through those last days, reading her favorite bible stories to her. The cancer was too advanced, and my beautiful sister passed away at the age of fifty.

Her favorite saying from the bible was "Be the Light." From the moment she passed, I vowed to fulfill that legacy.

And so, my life has forever changed. I finally saw that all my cracks have divine purpose. I finally realized how all the experiences, all the people encountered, had a higher calling for my life. I finally understood that the cracks in my crystal ball made me perfectly imperfect to fulfill that purpose. My crystal ball became even more beautiful as I bonded those split seams with purpose, light, and hope. My crystal ball can now, once again, sparkle and shine, not only in sunlight but even when darkness falls.

Pamela Fenili is an empowerment and results coach and mentor with a proven track record of inspiring hundreds of people over the past five years in transforming themselves in body, mind, and finances. She offers a solutions-oriented approach for those who want to level up in *all* areas of their lives by prioritizing their health and wellness. Pamela knows that when we feel our best, we show up better in every relationship, personal and professional. Pamela coaches by lending clients some of her confidence while teaching them to build their own from the inside out. She loves partnering with those who want to grow in all areas, knowing that life wellness begins with the relationships we have with ourselves.

Nicole Gaither

Shift Happens

The words failed to flow. A week past the due date for my initial rough draft, I was still determining where to start or how to finish. I only knew I had to convey the message about the inner power accessible by all: the power of who we are. That a shift was possible at any moment if we believed it possible.

Who am I to talk about an inner power? I thought.

I texted a dear friend about this not-yet-a-chapter, "I haven't done anything. It's a story of empowerment, a pivotal moment that has changed and transformed our lives." There have been so many "key" moments . . .

How was I to demonstrate the power of the present moment? What would allude to and get you, the reader, to question the reality in which you live? What can I say to remind others of your innate internal navigational system that we call feelings? How would I show you, my reader, the power of thought and your ability to change your life with your ideas, if you should see fit? After all, I was given a fifteen-hundred-word limit. How do I repackage the message, gifted to me, to give to you, in about two hundred and fifty lines of text?

We are all powerful simply because we exist. Look no further than to find a pulse if you're wondering whether you have a purpose in life.

We each operate from an internal navigational system to help guide our actions. We notice indicators such as, Do I feel good when I do this? Where am I in pain? How much anxiety am I feeling right now? Is it right for me? Is it the right size, energy, or a good fit?

For me, the question is this straightforward, and the answer of fewer than ten words is familiar. But for others, how can fifteen hundred words convey the power we all contain?

I recall the little green house I grew up in in a poverty-stricken neighborhood. I remember looking out my grandmother's upstairs bedroom as a young girl and focusing on the bridge that crossed the barely visible water in the distance. And I remember wanting to be by that river.

I thought often, *How wonderful would it be to live right by the river?* Then, when I was ten years old, my family moved near the great Mississippi River. My front door was just a five-minute walk from that river I had longed to be close to.

And then there was my desire to win a Publishers Clearing House sweepstake and the shock I felt when I *did* win one. How good it felt to receive that $1,000 check in the mail!

By paying attention to my feelings and following cues from my internal navigation system, I continued to manifest such wishes as I grew. When I first attended classes at the Southern Illinois University campus for my bachelor's in Psychology, I found it peaceful and beautiful. I imagined how excellent and convenient housing on campus would be. And then came the blessed moment when I accepted the keys to my three-bedroom apartment, home for me, my son, and my German Shepherd.

Finally, I remember my commitment to my beautiful 2014 Hyundai Elantra. At first, I felt fear when I applied for the loan. I recall showing the prospective car to a friend and her exclaiming that it was ugly! But *I knew*. I said, "No, this is a perfect car. This car is for me. It's a stick shift.

It's pretty. This is my car." And I drove that car for quite some time. I now own a custom-made 2022 Ford Bronco. When I was younger, my dad had a blue one, and I said when I got big, I would get one just like him. I'm big now, and I have it, but black, not blue.

But do I want to tell you that this is all my inner guidance is for? Should the chapter only be about all those times I asked and received? Or should I also talk about the darker times?

Do I tell of the broken-hearted sixteen-year-old who acquired vodka, drank it alone after her family slept, and used Capri Suns to chase it? The teen who took sleeping pills…a lot. It was a short phase of experimenting with risk, taking ten tablets and then trying to stay awake. One of the riskiest episodes was when at school.

Or do I let you see my eighteen-year-old self? Thinking yet again that I was in love, I found a lover who loved another, whose name was Opiate. Opiates became my lover as well, but I was able to break up with that relationship. The boy I left behind never did. Opiate changed who she was to him—even went by a different name, fentanyl—but the boy who is now a man…I don't know him at all.

Or do I take you back to the crack house when I was nineteen? What about rehab? Maybe the sharing of that experience would deliver my message. Trying to pinpoint the exact moment that I stopped worrying about everyone else and started focusing on myself is difficult. When *did* I stop listening to society and listen to myself? When did I stop using other people's transgressions as an excuse to cope with my own?

What was the exact day that I accepted myself fully? In which moment did I decide to love others unconditionally regardless of the outcome?

"I am procrastinating," I texted my friend. "It's hard to talk about self-empowerment, the beauty of life, and how we are all powerful creators, when I'm creating what I'm creating right now."

My dear friend responded, "Talk about it." She advised that I needed to share the shadow with readers too "because the world needs vulnerability." My friend continued, "Empowerment isn't only about the good. It's about honoring the in-between moments and slowing down to reflect and realign. We need to know that it is OK to embrace the moments that didn't work. And we need to remember that when things don't work out as we wanted them, they still serve a purpose."

So…here goes. I am writing this from my house, which is valued beyond what I expected it to be at this point. It is up the street from where I grew up in subsidized housing. And when I was little, I said, "When I get big, I'm going to live in a rich people's house up the street."

Here I am. Here I am. And yet…

In the same world where I created two beautiful children, in the same world where I drive my custom 2022 Bronco, where I live in my fancy house with my hot tub and my garage, and three different porches on eleven acres, I have allowed and expanded chaos.

I decided to go to school for a master's program, and I'm still unsure how I feel about one key feature. I am supposed to follow a system mainly guided by the *Diagnostic and Statistical Manual of Mental Disorders (DSM-5-TR)*, written by psychiatrists, of whom 70 percent are affiliated with pharmaceutical companies. And I noticed significant gaps in the *DSM*. No book could teach someone what to say to a mother grieving over losing her child who has just overdosed. No book can show a teacher how to reach the unreachable and unteachable children.

They're using their intuition. They're using their gut. They're accessing their higher selves. That's not being talked about, and it needs to be.

We're not taught to listen to ourselves. Perhaps that's why there are so many injustices committed against children, because they are expected to listen to the *more significant* people, They learn that more prominent people—the ones in charge—know everything.

But how many know what it's like to be the child who's had something happen to them—knowing it didn't feel right—but they thought they couldn't go somewhere, they couldn't tell somebody? Their adult selves live with these secrets because someone in authority said it was what they should be doing, and they went along with it instead of trusting their gut.

Because children aren't taught to trust their guts, they're reared to trust adults in charge, so most of us don't know how to trust ourselves. Perhaps that's why polls and surveys show that many people are unsatisfied with their jobs and marriages, with the latter failing. Not only do we have new DSM-V diagnoses for our problems, but we also have new pills for old and new diagnoses.

Reclaiming the ability to listen to our inner wisdom does not occur suddenly in a magical moment. There is no pivotal turning point. Returning to your guidance system is a moment-by-moment progression of believing that stagnation doesn't last. Our power to change is always in the now. It is a matter of going within, deciding that you want something, and believing it will come true. It's about cultivating belief in yourself when no one else seems to have any. The same magic that beats our hearts causes the sun and the moon to follow their paths.

This magic is something we all have access to simply by existing. When we are ready to stop disconnecting ourselves from our limiting beliefs, when we are ready to stop listening to those who say we cannot or should not, we will listen to what we are being called to do. Then, we will learn to flow into our feelings rather than to the flow around us.

In every moment of my life thus far, good or bad, there was a choice to continue down the path I could see easily or to take the road less traveled. Either way, a shift is possible, and a change can happen.

Nicole Gaither holds a certificate of Proficiency in Early Childhood Development and an Associate of Science obtained from Lewis and Clark Community College. She is a certified Reiki practitioner and earned a bachelor's in Psychology from Southern Illinois University–Edwardsville. Nicole completed her master's in Social Work in 2023 and is a certified life coach, acknowledged by the International Coaching Federation (IFC). She is projected to be a shaman by the end of 2023, according to the standards in the Peruvian Shamanic Cross-Cultural Medicine Wheel Program offered by the Center for Personal Evolution. She lives happily with her handsome son, Theoren, beautiful daughter, Nova, and dog-son, Dyer Allen.

Tabatha Baker

God's Timing

Do you know what it is like to wonder who your parents really are? Brought into this world by a young, unwed girl of sixteen who was numbed with drugs and alcohol, I'd learned fear, through life's abuse, by the age of five: fear of asking questions or standing up for myself. Unlike other children my age, I was not even a *little* inquisitive. My young parents had already married and divorced by that time, and I lived with my grandparents.

That same year, my dad, Rodney, died in a car accident. A year later, one of his family introduced me to someone as "Rodney's stepdaughter." I vividly remember that surprising label and recall the feeling in my stomach. I knew that term *stepdaughter*, but in my young mind it meant not real. Emotionally, I again felt the same devastation as when hearing that my dad had gone to heaven.

Back home, out of sorts, sad, and scared to ask or talk about it, I didn't want to hurt my grandma or anger my mom by asking about dad. A week later, during some alone time with my Aunt Sharon, I found my opportunity. After lunch, snuggling with her on the couch, and feeling safe and full of trust, I asked, "Why would Aunt Jetty call me Rodney's stepdaughter?"

I don't remember her facial expression, just the sadness and concern in her voice. "Do you know what that means?" she asked, and I answered,

"Yeah, that he's not really my dad." She replied that he loved me and was my daddy...and then changed the subject.

On my next visit with Mom, she turned off my Saturday morning cartoons and sat next to me on the couch. I remember feeling uneasy; even at that age I had already learned that when adults "need to talk," it was always painful. She said, "I know you learned that Rodney was your stepdad." I froze as she went on asking if I knew what that meant, and I nodded. She affirmed what my aunt had said: he loved me like I was his child, but I really wasn't.

Shakily, I asked, "Then who is my real dad?" In the next few minutes, I learned his name and that, in her eyes, my bio dad was a cute country-rock guitarist she crushed on, and that "it" just happened in the back seat of a car. She also shared the details she remembered: he went to Windsor High School and flew airplanes.

As she continued, I learned that, confronted, he had denied he could be the father. He had "never come around," she said, other than one attempt to abduct me when I was a toddler. I cried when she asked if I wanted to meet him and vividly remember both my grief and her words. That short list of details was all I had for the next forty years.

I was a mom of two young men, exiting my second failed marriage, and seeking who I am as a child of God. I felt ashamed, worthless, and as though I had hit rock bottom. With nearly nothing but a willingness to try, I finally began listening to the nudges God was placing in my heart for my safety, freedom, and future. The gift of a restart gave me permission to find my real dad! Letting go and healing from so much other devastation in my life, I saw that adding that search and getting past the need to know would be one less thing to deal with later.

Starting with Facebook, I found someone I was sure was him in just a few minutes! We had a similar smile, he was the right age, played guitar, flew airplanes. OK…here I jump! I sent a message, asking if he knew my mom from high school. After a few months with no response, I spoke to a few of Mom's long-time friends and an uncle. But nobody could affirm my best guess; everyone said she never talked about him.

Life continued, with many lessons, blessings, and much healing over the next few years. A new husband, childhood friends, a tremendous mentor, and an outpouring of opportunities continued to fuel the fire of curiosity about my biological father. I was nervous but continued to feel God's nudges to find him.

My youngest son, Justin, for his twenty-first birthday in 2022 asked for an ancestry DNA kit. "Hey, Mom, we can both do it for our birthdays?" "OK, son, sure," I said apprehensively. In fact, I resisted joining him until a friend texted me on my birthday, sharing an ad for fifty percent off an Ancestry test. This note from this fearless angel read, "It's your birthday and there's a sale!" God's nudge received; I bought our two tests for the price of one! Surely this would be my path to my dad.

But the results offered no helpful information. My friend who texted the discount then referred me to an agency called DNA Angels, which helps people locate birth parents. After hitting a few more stumbling blocks, their volunteer reached out to ask, "Did either of your parents go to Windsor High School?" Soon, she sent a yearbook photo of fourteen-year-old Bill Hartman, and I sent it back, paired with a picture of me from about the same age. That was enough confirmation for her, and she sent his contact information and the link to his Facebook profile.

And it was the same man I had messaged five years earlier.

The next few days were a blur of tearful and confusing emotions: joy, sadness, anger, and a lot of bitterness and resentment. After a week of supportive witnessing, my husband, Tom, on his own initiative, put a note on my father's door. Short and to the point, it opened a dialogue.

Questions asked and answered, there was a request for a picture of my mother. Finally, we learned we were texting with Debbie, Bill's wife, and therefore my stepmom. She shared Bill's concert schedule and invited me for a visit.

In a few weeks, when the shock had worn off, Tom and I went to hear Bill play. Debbie greeted us warmly, as did their friends and family who joined us. Then Bill played "New York, New York". His patter about loving the city and his favorite Italian restaurant there brought me another God moment: Frank Sinatra is one of my favorite singers, and I had just returned from New York.

I prayed and breathed through my anxiety, trusting and listening to the nudges in my heart of what to say and do. My last nudge arrived as the evening was wrapping up, as I watched a beautiful little girl with big, blue eyes and long, curly blonde hair watching Bill and wanting to dance but holding back. She beamed at my invitation to dance, and we spun, laughed, and danced away all my fear and anger. Only love and joy remained flowing, as Tom and I lingered for more conversation with Bill and Debbie before farewells.

As we left, there were many hugs, but the last of the evening was with Bill, my dad. I held back the tears and quivers, hugged him tightly, and said, "Please take care of you." His reply left the door open for us to see each other again, so I invited him to lunch the next week. We've continued to see each other almost weekly, and a beautiful father-daughter relationship has blossomed.

The small voice within, nudging each of us to do something, is God's guidance for a great lesson. I am still processing fear, anger, sadness, and jealousy at times, but I have had a wonderful support system, and my dad and bonus mama have been tremendous in the healing of my heart on this journey.

The biggest lesson I have learned and hope to also teach—or to regift by telling this story—is to trust, respond, and obey God's guidance; the good, the bad, and the ugly feelings all serve part of His purpose. He placed people, experiences, and opportunities along my path for a reason. I obeyed His guidance, with respect, and did all the things He nudged me to do. I trusted that the nudges God gives are for my good, and the good of others, as an example of His glory, and so it is!

Tabatha Baker is the Managing Director of Worth Living Wellness. A mentor and coach, she advocates for women who seek positive change and resources to live a life worthy of their calling. For almost five years, she has offered coaching, mentorship, and training in multiple modalities, with many options for healing and growth that women can explore to support their journeys. Tabatha is a Certified Health and Wellness Coach, Neuro-Linguistic Programming practitioner, timeline practitioner, Revelation Wellness Fitness instructor, and Certified Consulting Hypnotist. She offers individualized, intensive coaching programs, monthly Bible-based gatherings, and retreats on whole living. In addition to nurturing and working with women, she is a wife, mother, and Oma (grandmother). She enjoys riding motorcycles, traveling, and facing fears head on!

Paula Bubb Whiting

Growing Through What We Go Through

In my gut I knew I shouldn't have gone with him for a walk. I felt the fear begin to bubble up as he walked me down the hill by our home. That huge hill was the one we always sledded on in the winter and, up until that point, was a place of pure joy. He had his huge—and to my thought—ferocious dog with him, and I felt powerless.

When I realized no one else was coming with us, I felt tricked, and a little voice told me to turn around, but I didn't. After tying his dog up and asking me to sit on his lap, he tried to take off my clothes. I laughed a little, saying "stop that." My thoughts were abstract, randomly popping up with internal messages: *no, stop, run, kick, punch, scream.*

What had my parents said about strangers touching me? This man wasn't a stranger, though, so did that count? If I told him to stop, would he let his dog attack me? I felt myself above us, looking down, watching the whole thing play out. In the distance, I heard my mom and dad calling my name, and I remember saying, "My parents are calling me. I have to go."

I got up and started walking, then running up the hill, all the while feeling the terror that he was about to grab me and pull me back down, although he was still standing in the same place. He was shouting "Come back," and his dog was barking at me, but his shouts were fading, and my parents' frantic voices were getting louder. So I just kept running until I reached their arms. The magnitude of what happened, or what could have happened, didn't hit me until that point.

In the weeks that followed, we heard that I wasn't the only girl attacked in this way, and that some of the other assaults had been more traumatic than mine. I would have to go to court and tell my story. I didn't want to; I just wanted it all to go away.

Reliving it by retelling it was one of the worst parts, not to mention having to see my parents so upset because I was upset. My anxiety ramped up to extreme levels. I stuck to my mom like glue and didn't want to be out of sight of my home, even to play outside or go to a friend's house. I wanted everything to be OK, I didn't want people to feel sorry for me or like they had to tread lightly around me, because really, I was a strong girl who stood up for myself and others, or at least I had been until then.

Since then, I can't remember a time when I haven't felt fear and anxiety. I grew up in a military family, so I changed schools about every three years, living all over the United States and even overseas. That lifestyle was enough to plant those feelings. Add to that being taken by a neighbor and the trauma of the court experiences afterward, and I guess it created the perfect storm for fear and anxiety to grow and, at times, take over my life.

The summer of my ninth-grade year, my dad retired from the military and we settled in the town where I would graduate from high school, meet my husband, Clay, and make friends with some amazing people who have become more like family than friends. That feeling of acceptance and belonging felt amazing, by the way.

For many of those childhood years, I hadn't thought of myself as "anxious" or "fearful," perhaps because those feelings manifested in ways that could be considered normal. For example, I didn't want to go to sleepovers, or on fun trips with friends; I didn't want to stay home by myself. The most high-impact example was hiding behind the fear and not leaving my comfort zone when opportunities came my way.

Like singing. I love it and I'm good at it; it's my God-given gift. In my younger years I was always in choir; I loved singing with a group. That way I wasn't singing by myself, but I still got to sing. As I got older, I was asked to sing at events, and my first answer was always a firm "No!" In junior high and high school, I loved drama class, dance team, and choir. But I can't adequately describe the crippling anxiety I felt when asked to do a solo in either drama or choir. On dance team, I felt I had the talent to be Captain or Co-Captain, but anxiety always fed the self-doubt, keeping me from stepping out and believing in myself.

It was much the same in the other classes I loved; my desire to sing the solo or play the part was just as heavy on my heart as the anxiety. Even so, I would let the comfort win out when I knew I could have done it. I dreamed vividly about being on stage, feeling so proud of myself because I had done it, because I had said yes! But after waking up I would realize it was only a dream and I had said no. I participated in "reader's theater" events or in the chorus of musicals to stay in my comfort zone.

It wasn't until an amazing drama teacher—and friend to this day, Jane Balgavy (Morgan) —inspired me to step out a little more, taking a small part in a play that I helped write and singing a couple solos. The anxiety was still there, and crippling at times, but she taught me the art of focusing on a neutral point in the room rather than on all the people watching me. Because of that one lesson in focus, that dream of the spotlight came true, increasing my confidence.

Several years after I graduated high school and Clay graduated college, we got married and welcomed two beautiful children. Becoming a wife and mother was what I always wanted to do. Marrying my high school sweetheart...well, he's the best thing that has ever happened to me. It's hard for him to understand my fear and anxiety because he's a natural extrovert and loves to speak, whether he's at work, church, or just out with friends. He has shared his testimony or given reports at church in the past, before which I'd strongly stated that he was not to include me. Still, "no" was my first answer in such situations.

Five years ago, I started a weight-loss program, and when Clay decided to join me, I became a health coach. It was beyond my vision, back then, that this new role would be the catalyst for huge change in my life. I began to not only shed physical weight but a lifetime of mental and emotional weight as well.

At a conference with hundreds of other health coaches, our speaker said something that changed everything for me. "This isn't your practice life!" Five simple words that literally flipped a switch inside me. I remember thinking, "I could do and be so much more!" So I left that conference inspired to do just that.

I initiated more practices for personal development and growing self-awareness of my thoughts and their impact on my behavior. When I was asked to speak at trainings, or on panels at conferences, I said yes! What did I really have to lose? The pounds off my body were a relief, but releasing the burdens on my heart and mind was transformative. I also realized that when I said yes to sharing my heart and passion, it was very well received. At a recent conference, I learned that I had inspired a peer to step out and be bold because I had done it, another feeling of significant completion.

Someone said to me once that "changed lives *change* lives," and that became my mantra. My thinking began to shift. Looking back, the life transitions that flowed from my role as a health coach were really "a God thing." When the quarantines started, my company sent us all home to work. I loved it and wanted to be able to do that indefinitely. My first grandbaby was on his way, and I saw that health coaching could offer me the freedom I needed to provide daily care for him. I'd had to enroll both of my children in child care at six weeks of age, which absolutely broke my heart! As a health coach, I could provide at-home care for my grandchild, as I had longed to with my own children. Now I have three grands and I love being a Gigi!

Through all these decades of growth and change, I've found that I'm not alone in my trauma. I have friends, family, and acquaintances who survived similar experiences. Telling my story removes my focus from my feelings of anxiety and fear and directs my emotional energy toward the more positive outcome of helping others. Committing to my own steps to get healthy—mentally and physically—enabled me to grow personally. I can be bold, take chances, continue to step out of my comfort zone, and live my life out loud, unapologetically, and with purpose. My wish for anyone reading my story is to realize they, too, can find purpose through pain.

Paula Bubb Whiting is a Christian, a wife, a mom, a beloved Gigi, a health and wellness coach, and loves to motivate and inspire others. After releasing twenty-five pounds and reclaiming her health, Paula realized her passion for serving others and walking beside them on their journeys to wellness. Paula made the decision to coach full time because it allowed freedom to spend time with her grandchildren. Married to her high school sweetheart, Clay, for thirty-three years, they've raised two amazing children who are now both married to their own loves, and parents to the sweetest babies ever born.

Heather L. Kemper

From Shadows to Self-Love: Owning Your Story

The challenge with memories is that if you don't own them, others etch them in their own ink. Thoughts become distorted, altered, and deeply woven into a narrative that may not reflect your truth.

Shadows of your past may threaten to define your future.

My youth was a tapestry woven of simpler threads. I remember stirring sweet Neapolitan ice cream in a bowl, homecoming fairs filled with lights and duck ponds, and an unending pile of stuffed animals hiding me like E.T. And yet there were instances that seemed like mere shadows, but would later take a solid, haunting form. In a home with both love and longing, I learned early that memories can take on a life of their own within a young, untamed mind.

One memory remains vivid. In a world that smelled of elementary innocence, my mother, with hard-liquored breath, let out an echoing scream toward the orange, crushed-velvet recliner. My father sat there, a silhouette in cigarette smoke, accepting his title as "betrayer of promises." From this slight fissure in our familial tapestry, we tore apart.

The steadiness I once felt became a jagged terrain as multiple men entered and exited our mommy-me sphere. And then she found the darkest shadow of them all: a man who was anything but a refuge.

Home, they say, is where one finds comfort. But what if that very sanctuary morphs into a theater of echoes and screams? Recollections of blush-colored prom dresses and teenage angst were now juxtaposed with dread, seclusion, and frequent visits from the police to our doorstep. This man, my stepfather, stripped my mother of her value, diminishing her into a person I no longer recognized.

My adolescent years armored me as I simply watched our smoke-discolored walls bear the impact of his fury, glass lie like fallen stars on the faux wooden floors, and the beige phone dangle, broken from its perch. Even when he took my mother's long, permed hair into his mechanic-dirty hands and twisted her down to the floor as crimson red dripped from her lips, I stood by, stiffly mute. Was his punishment for an overdone meal? A tardy beer? Or was it the defense of her child? I still don't remember the "why."

The edges of memories are often reshaped by trauma, blurred by the haze of our need to escape overwhelming pain and horror. Yet their fluctuating images still etch indelible marks upon our minds, seeming just as real and true as happy memories. I still grapple with the clarity of these recollections: Did she do something to deserve his backlash? Did she really ever rise in my defense? And even as these questions dance on the periphery of my mind, contradictory scenes rush to the center: the sting of her open hand on my cheek, the weight of her body pinning me down on the floor as the ever-present hum of the refrigerator bore silent witness, her voice mixing maternal care and sharp rebuke.

The ensuing years, a whirlwind of growth and grit, saw me embrace the sanctity of motherhood. However, just as I was immersing myself in this new role, the shadows of the past reached back out. My mother's body began a slow betrayal. Whispers of cancer, while the man beside her turned a blind eye, refusing to ensure she received the proper care. I still yearn today for my memories to affirm that, as the cruel disease journeyed from her organs to her mind, I championed her cause the best I could, just as she did for me in my early childhood days, before our first family tore apart. I remember being so distressed after consulting a lawyer about seeking guardianship, which proved fruitless. Her husband's hold was too tight.

Then one day the phone rang, its shrill tone echoing the dread I felt. I predicted this moment and felt torn: should I feel a grim satisfaction at my intuition of the illness leading her to the hospital, or anger at his neglect that let her condition deteriorate to this extent? In the emergency room, none of that mattered in the face of the overpowering scent of clinical sterility punctuated with undertones of sorrow.

The first thing I noticed was her skin, sickly yellow and marred with bruises. The weight of choices bore down as I was named the decision-maker: was it time to let go, for her body to finally be free? As the chaos of the emergency room surged and flowed around us, the man who'd cast the darkest shadow over her life sat hunched in a corner. His voice, for once, was silenced. As the machines maintained their relentless rhythms, I wrestled with the impending end of her life and the dark predictions I felt it held for my own.

Grief has a peculiar texture. It envelops, constricts, yet somehow liberates.

My mother's ending tore my illusions of my own "happy" relationship. The dark parallels between her life and mine were stark and undeniable. In her narrative, I glimpsed the potential path of my own, if I were to let my current abusive relationship hold me captive.

The realization was as sharp as the cold air in that hospital room. Her tragic demise served as an ominous beacon—a warning light on the life that I was living. I understood then that her final lesson to me wasn't in her living, but in her passing.

Truly seeing myself for the first time, I came to the stark realization that if I remained in my brokenness—if I kept nurturing the notion that I was undeserving of more than the toxic union I was trapped in—I'd follow my mother's footsteps.

Still, I didn't walk away from the relationship immediately. My mother's tragic end was an eye-opener, uncovering a vast canvas of my surrounding reality—the way I was seen, touched, and belittled showed up in stark contrast to the respect and love I yearned for and unknowingly deserved. But I didn't understand how to change my trajectory.

My pursuit of knowledge took me to seminary school, where a course on forgiveness became a mirror. True forgiveness, I realized, wasn't mere words, but was anchored in genuine transformation—a transformation glaringly absent from the relationship. The barbed words, the disdainful gestures, the violations—all too reminiscent of my mother's marriage that I allowed to frame my thoughts on how I was to be treated by a man. Yet with every new verbal and physical assault, my mother's light from above shone down, dispersing past shadows, spotlighting that "love" is more than what I was experiencing.

Finally, the last day my partner's darkness imprinted itself on my skin, as crimson red dripped from my own lips, I found, deep within, the courage to reach out for the lifeline I had so long denied myself.

"911, what's your emergency?"

What's my emergency?? If I were to share my inner responses, I'd hardly know where to begin. My emergency is that I am a middle-aged woman, with three children who depend on me asleep upstairs. My mother is dead. My career is nonexistent. I have a past that constantly overwhelms my thoughts, sending me into self-loathing fits, and, oh… my "love" just hit me again and won't leave, so I've locked myself in a bathroom. *Is that enough emergencies?*

Back in the echoing silence of my childhood home, I had often yelled out, yearning for a response from the unyielding walls. I wrote until my fingers ached, the pages bearing witness to a voice that seemed unheard by any ears. I had resigned myself to a life of quiet submission, awaiting direction.

But as the 911 operator answered, the dried blood of his fury still stuck to my face, I felt a divine nudge, a clear message: *it was time to free myself.*

Rebuilding my self-worth wasn't without its battles. Memories and echoing tales of lies reframed as truth threatened to pull me back into suffocating self-doubt. That onslaught of inward skepticism was relentless: Would I truly be alright on my own? Was I really strong enough to forge this new path? *Would anyone else love me?*

And it was that final reflection that bore the most weight.

I realized that my journey toward healing required a deep dive into self-exploration, which I embarked upon through therapy. This process involved shedding the layers of labels and descriptions that others had imposed upon me over the years, to uncover the essence of my true self. Through this journey, I developed a clearer understanding of the dynamics that led both my mother and myself to endure such treatment from those who claimed to "love" us. This understanding illuminated the reasons behind our acceptance of such degrading behavior. It was a pivotal moment for me to realize that my primary objective needed to be self-love: a complete acceptance and embrace of my imperfections, a courageous confrontation of my innermost demons, and a celebration of my strengths and accomplishments.

This mission was not just about healing old wounds but also about empowering myself to create a brighter, healthier future.

Today, I immerse myself in life's simple wonders, finding peace in the sun's embrace during woodland hikes, the gentle serenades of water while kayaking, or the simple giggles of my children. Through my mother's loss,

I unearthed my inner voice and emerged from the shadows, resilient with the innate power that guides *my* narrative.

I am not trash. I am not a little bitch. I am not a failure. I am not an embarrassment.

I am imperfect. I am a work in progress. However, I am love and I am loved by those who truly see me and, most importantly, by myself.

When I find my mind ensnared in distorted memories, I try to remember that I wield the quill of my destiny. Realizing that I am worthy of love, I now own the power to transform past pain into my own enduring tale of resilience, hope, and redemption—*a story my mother would be proud of.*

Heather L. Kemper | From Shadows to Self-Love: Owning Your Story

Heather L. Kemper, MFA, CFRE, ACNP, is not just a seasoned nonprofit professional; she's an advocate for philanthropy, inspired by the ripple of impact it creates and the deep joy it infuses into the lives of others. A proud graduate of the University of Missouri–Columbia and Lindenwood University, her academic pursuits also saw a year at seminary. Crowned Mrs. Missouri America in 2016, she journeyed across her state, championing inner beauty and civic duty. Her trophy shelf boasts awards like Beyond the Best, ATHENA Young Professional Leadership, and Unsung Hero. However, her crowning achievement is motherhood—raising three spirited children, nurturing their emotions, and navigating the challenging, joyous journey of parenthood. Heather's expertise lies in catalyzing revenue avenues for both nonprofits and businesses, underpinned by her unwavering belief in philanthropy's transformative power.

Deanna Rose

Then the Miracle

That I am here with peace, purpose, and joy in my soul is a miracle.

Disintegrate

She's gone.
Her body is in the morgue, cold, white, bloody, alone.
A tag on her chubby big toe.
We had laughed at our matching chubby toes.
She left.
How did this happen?
She wanted to live.
Oh, how I failed her.
I would give my life for her a million times over.
Disintegrate.
Cease to exist.
Be gone, Deanna.
Deanna is not going to disintegrate.
Oh God, why? Why not?
Please, please let me disappear.
Let this be an illusion. A nightmare.
Spontaneous human combustion. Focus on it. Make it happen. Go away.
*I'm not going to combust. F**k this unjust, unfair, cruel world.*
*F**k you for making her pain so great. For not helping her.*

Surrounded with men who think she exists to serve them. Whose neglect and selfishness hurt her.
F**k mold and Lyme disease.
Why my sweet girl?
I cannot hate anymore.
Scream, cry, gasp. Sleep. Work the anger and despair out of my body. Good luck with that.
What is left?
I cannot leave my family on life support, gasping for air. Struggling to live.
I give in. I give up. My body breathes. My eyes see. My ears hear.
I am stuck here.
And then, the miracle unfolded.

A Perfect Storm

In 2015, the "I" that I knew died the moment I learned my beautiful nineteen-year-old daughter pulled the trigger. What I know now is that the "I" who was lost created room for the "I" of today—the one God created me to be.

Toxic mold exposure and its effects, the suicide of our beloved Amanda Rose, and betrayal hit my family and hit hard. *Hard* is a weak word for the resulting trauma. Our move to the San Francisco Bay Area led to this "perfect storm."

Behind the pretty walls of our rented home, and in the air ducts, a poison grew. It started a cascade of confounding health issues in my daughters: seizures, headaches, nerve pain, debilitating fatigue, chest pains, vomiting, random fainting, hair loss, panic attacks, depression, digestive pain, autonomic dysfunction, hallucinations, personality changes, anxiety, and suicidal "thought intrusions." We constantly found ourselves in doctors' offices or the ER.

As a mother, I fought to get help for my girls, and struggled watching them suffer. Shock and dismay came over us as we had difficulty getting real help. My girls were forced to give up school, sports, and social life when they could barely get out of bed some days. Most of the drugs prescribed only exacerbated symptoms or led to new ones. A functional medicine doctor finally directed us to accurate information and confirmation that hidden mold was the catalyst for so much illness and chaos.

To protect our immune systems, we immediately left our home and most of our belongings. Willing to do anything necessary to prevent our girls' suffering, we moved repeatedly, seeking a "clean" place to heal. The years of exposure and struggle took a brutal toll not only on our daughters but on us, the parents whose trauma and illness manifested in different ways. However, just as it seemed we were beginning the climb out of mold hell, the unfathomable happened.

In a single moment, we lost our radiantly beautiful, tough, loving Amanda Rose. I forgave her, knowing she carried too much. She pulled the trigger in a moment of sheer overwhelm, of impulse control lost. It was much more difficult for me to forgive myself than it was to forgive her. I may have failed to protect her, to see the signs, to help her discover tools prior to the storm, to help her navigate a fallen world. But our love for each other never failed.

Within the darkness of the storm, I saw the light; the many truths of which I had been unaware…and I forgave myself.

Beauty from Ashes

How does a mother survive her child's death by suicide, let alone thrive and feel joy again? Through *love*. I love my daughter, she loves me, and we both know it, still. Love's stubborn presence and survival through the messy and imperfect is what makes it real and true.

That love was tangible and at work through a divine intervention that opened my eyes to God and the eternal nature of our souls. God laid the foundation for my healing by enabling contact with Amanda: amazing signs kept me alive with glimpses of hope and joy through the despair. Amanda Rose contacted me repeatedly in the first few months after her passing; I heard her sweet voice on four occasions, at first questioning myself.

In those early days, I woke up every morning to the nightmare, gasping and filled with terror. Then one morning a warm, powerful peace washed over me. Suddenly I was on a beautiful ocean beach at sunset, with Rosie standing at the water's edge in a lovely lace dress, holding a little bouquet of roses and smiling at me over her shoulder, her curly hair gently moving in the breeze. Our souls met three more times on that beach, and each encounter was tangible, powerful, and filled with meaning. She had not left us.

I saw another message in a single, perfect red rose that grew tall in the center of one bush among a group that usually all bloomed together in our backyard. She stood in that very same spot for a family photo a few years before. I found single dimes (well over one hundred to this day), the placement and timing of these messages as uncanny as they are clear and inspirational.

Between these healing visits and signs, I felt God's presence as I screamed, sobbed, choked, and raged. Feeling and accepting my emotions released the pain from my body and helped me balance myself one breath, one small step, after another. The ultimate test was to somehow love myself the way I loved others. People, lessons, and events were all placed before me to help forge my way. I asked for and accepted help from therapists, coaches, bereaved parents, family, and friends. I learned that few were willing or able to navigate such trauma and pain, yet I found my "tribe," those I could rely on, who would not shrink back.

I practiced discernment as I responded and reacted in my new world. I learned that some people I loved and trusted did not love me. I let go of what and who drained my energy and immersed myself in everything healing and restorative. I asked myself, with every thought or emotion I had, every bite of food, everything I did or did not do: "Is this adding to or taking away from my health?" And I adjusted accordingly.

That persistent voice within also guided me to ardently seek answers about what really happened to my daughter. I tenaciously pursued knowledge about health, toxic mold, infectious disease, the environment, drugs, food, and trauma. I studied methods of resilience and learned powerful ways to heal and thrive that didn't require a doctor. I examined my strengths and weaknesses and worked with them in mind. I read the stories of parents who lost children to suicide, connected to, and leaned on them, and they leaned on me too. I learned from those who have experienced toxic mold illness and chronic infection. I dove into the deep, cleansing waters of healing.

While navigating all these layers of a new reality, I wrote to Amanda in a journal I bought just for her. I promised to laugh and smile for her every day, to be grateful that she was earthside for nineteen years and *soulside* forever. I promised to make the best of a confounding and painful journey by sharing the lessons we learned. Those promises keep me determined to persevere.

Passion and Purpose

Amanda Rose's love and light continues to shine in my life, and in the lives of many who know her. She is not defined by her last moments but by the blessing she is, and the lessons she left. Her last moments, however, revealed how desperately the world needs greater understanding. We all need to ask ourselves: What can I learn? What can be done differently? How can we all do better? These are the questions that ignite passion and purpose within me, and I am obligated to share.

As I rebuilt my life after the storm and the trauma that followed, it prepared me for yet another great pain and loss: betrayal and divorce. It was the third "bomb" dropped on my family after toxic mold exposure and the suicide death of Amanda. It could have been the straw that crushed me. But I realized as I observed, anguished, and learned, that it was saving grace.

Now, against all odds, I love life even when it's not lovable. One sign, one breath, one lesson at a time, I was led to the renewal of my life and soul. As a mother, I survived and even thrived through what I thought was impossible. I discovered who I am and found peace and joy on the other side of suffocating tragedy. I am grateful to have had blessings worthy of such pain and grief.

I know how to detox and nourish my body, mind, and soul, and I learned that some of the simplest practices are powerful healers. I set boundaries and strive for authenticity and integrity; readjusting when I slip and knowing that God and grace are my safety net when I fall. By God's amazing grace and my stubborn participation in discovery, I see the lessons in most everything. At the end of the day, my soul is eternal, and there is purpose and peace to be found, even in the darkest moments. This is my miracle.

Known for late arrivals, Deanna's early appearance in 1966 foretold an active and productive life. A sweet upbringing at Lake Tahoe and a Bachelor of Science in Real Estate from California State University, Sacramento, preceded her 1990 marriage. Raising three daughters and supporting an ambitious husband led Deanna to prioritize her work as wife and mother. She evolved as vice president for family business, serving as accountant, beautician, cook, chauffeur, contract negotiator, school volunteer, pet caretaker, gardener, laundress, maid, nurse, party planner, psychologist, shopper, social worker, sports mom, cheerleader, referee, scheduler, teacher, waitress, and consultant. After life-altering hardships including the trauma of mold poisoning and its effects, a precious child's death, and eventual divorce, Deanna now shares the lessons she learned, as a life coach specializing in grief, suicide, and chronic illness. Knowing that no one wants to face those experiences, she is determined they will not face them alone.

Pooja Arshanapally

The Strength in Silence

Every word mattered, but at that moment they all seemed to escape my mind. I stood there, frozen, desperately trying to find the right words as they eluded me. Time seemed to stretch. I desperately grasped the fragments of my speech, trying to piece them together, but they slipped through my mind like a gush of wind. Each passing moment intensified the weight of my embarrassment, a heavy burden I couldn't escape.

In this speaking competition, every second counts, and I had just wasted thirty of them. Knowing I would be docked down in a ranking, I felt hopeless about moving forward. Now I was just standing there in utter silence, frantically trying to grasp the words I once knew.

Being silent wasn't usually a problem for me. In fact, I was used to it, being quiet to a fault. At every parent-teacher conference, I was considered the problem child. It wasn't like I was causing trouble or being a class clown. But I was extremely quiet and didn't participate in class. I was known as a deep concern to my teachers.

I think sometimes, because I was so quiet, teachers forgot that I was there. In middle school during science class, I nervously stepped up to deliver a speech. My voice barely audible, so soft, and almost fragile. It was a pivotal moment for the teacher because he suddenly realized he had made a mistake. Right in front of me, he went back to each student who'd delivered their speech before me and updated their grades. Because my voice was so soft, I'd reset the curve in the grades.

A wave of embarrassment washed over as the realization sank in. And because I had heard what the teacher was saying, I knew everyone in the classroom also knew why the grades shifted.

But this problem didn't just stay at school; it followed me everywhere. People couldn't seem to grasp the idea of someone who is quiet. Daily, there was the annoyance of people commenting about how quiet I was and giving unsolicited advice on how I should speak more. But the truth is, I had nothing to say and I was fine with that.

Sometimes, others got more hostile. Family, friends, and even strangers would stop their conversations, purposely waiting for my contribution to the conversation, and if I didn't contribute, I got scolded. People learned quickly, though, that I wasn't going to budge. Therefore, I didn't speak, and there was just awkward silence.

I tend to use silence as a shield. But sometimes that shield fell short. I remember at the age of ten, I heard that I wouldn't be a good mother. "How can you raise a family if you don't talk?" If someone told me this now, I would simply brush it off. But when you are so young, the people around you influence you. So I believed I would fail as a mother before I even knew what motherhood was about. I just knew being a mother wasn't a part of my life.

It wasn't until later that I realized how much misunderstanding there is about people who are soft-spoken and quiet. Deep down, I always knew who I was. But the constant pressure to speak up and initiate conversation was draining. It was exhausting to abide by other people's expectations of what they wanted me to be.

And yes, for some people, being pressured may help them speak. But for me it did the opposite. I didn't want to speak at all, and I made the conscious effort to resist what others wanted from me. It was my way of taking back my control.

I may have been in control, but at the same time I was isolated and an outsider. It wasn't until my sophomore year of high school that all of that seemed to change. My English teacher was the speech coach, too, but not for debate. His coaching was for the type of speech team where you get to perform. The prior year's seniors had graduated, so he was on a mission to recruit new members to compete. And for those who didn't have the pleasure of meeting my English teacher, he was a very persistent man.

He eyed us all like a hawk, keenly observing his surroundings, waiting for this opportunity to strike. Right when the bell rang, it was his cue to initiate a conversation with the next student. Regardless of who this person was, he would deliver the same speech: "[Name], I know you would be the perfect person to join my speech team!"

The students shook their heads and hastily made their way to the next class. Some would give in, and some would say no. But he always persisted. One by one, my teacher went down the line, and I knew it was my time. When he approached me, I was flustered; I didn't speak a word in his class! In that moment, I only managed to say "I'll think about it" to buy myself time.

I'd spent my whole life trying to fight against the obligations to talk in conversations. But before I rejected the offer, I realized I feared public speaking without having any experience at it. I realized the effects it might have, to shut out public speaking out of my life entirely: it would limit me. So I decided to step outside my comfort zone and try public speaking.

My teacher gave me the task to present a speech based on the book *Quiet* by Susan Cain. It spoke about the power of introverts, and it was the perfect topic to suit me. Therefore, I felt an enormous amount of pressure to do the speech justice, because it was about me.

Through the process of delivering this speech, I realized I was not good. I was too scared of making a fool of myself. Every time I practiced in front of a coach, I was frustrated by the awareness that I sucked! Learning to be a speaker automatically means you have to fail in front of people while they critique your underwhelming performance.

Also, delivering a speech is not just about memorizing and delivering lines, but about influencing the people in the room. It was not enough to memorize words; I had to learn how to emphasize the right words and get the pacing exactly right, such as knowing when to pause for effect. All these techniques fully engage the audience in what I have to share. I have learned to create an experience, to make my listeners feel they are with me in every sentence.

But I didn't know all this back in high school. My fixation on perfectionism led me to memorize my speech without enough practice, and I dreaded the possibility of forgetting my lines. However, as it turned out, the energy I put into the world came back to me in an unexpected way.

As I stepped to the stage to deliver the speech, a wave of nervousness washed over me. For the first few minutes I was doing fine, but as I reached the midpoint of my speech, a sudden panic entered my mind. I had forgotten the next sentence. All eyes fixed on me, waiting for me to finish my sentence, but words failed me. In a brief moment, I had this sinking feeling that the people who criticized me were right. I hit rock bottom.

But the funny thing is, hitting rock bottom wasn't as bad as I thought it was going to be. I realized at that moment I had nothing to prove. So I began the speech from where I last recalled and continued on.

When I stepped into that high school English class on the first day, I did not anticipate the size of the impact my teacher would have on my life. When so many people in your life have misconceptions about you, having someone who believes in and accepts you is truly life changing. That experience on the speech team was a catalyst for decisions I have made today. Now I can speak comfortably in front of crowds…and I did not have to change myself to do it. During that year, I found my voice and stopped allowing other people to speak for me.

Pooja Arshanapally is the founder of The Novus, where she helps authors market their books to give them access to more opportunities. From an early age, she recognized the profound truth that once you acquire knowledge, it can never be taken away. Recognizing that potential, she now devotes herself to helping authors harness the power of books as lead generators, using a well-positioned book to open doors to exciting possibilities and to make a lasting impact.

Rachel Boone

Rekindle Your Spark

Watching from afar, I admire how brightly she illuminates the space as she floats across the lawn. So beautiful. So vibrant. But admiring from a distance is not enough. I must have her, hold her, admire her close-up. With a swift motion, I catch her. In the jar, her light begins to dim. She is suffocating. Stuck inside the glass.

Just like the lightning bugs I used to catch when I was little, I found my light slowly dimming when I became a wife and a mother of four. I felt suffocated by family duties, work deadlines, and the never-ending list of tasks, requests, and responsibilities. Without even noticing it, my radiance gradually and quietly transformed into a soft light…until one day it was almost gone.

"Where did your light go?" a client asked me. "You don't seem the same as when we started working together three years ago. As if your spark has left."

What people needed me to do, I did. Who I needed to be, I became. I assumed the roles that I believed I was required to play without a second thought. I was caught, not in one container like my little lightning bug, but in many. Spread so thin and slowly running out of air. I was holding everything together, feeling alone, and I desperately yearned for my partner to resolve my cries for help, which were falling on deaf ears.

A shift began to occur when I realized my glow was fading. A transformation took place when I made the decision to reclaim forgotten aspects of myself and advocate for the kind of life I desired.

Gradually I opened the lids to all the glass jars containing me. Similar to a butterfly emerging from its chrysalis, I had to strengthen my wings. I craved the freedom to soar beyond the constraints of a flawless reputation and embrace vulnerability. I needed to challenge the notion that a child must unquestioningly listen to their parents. I had to break away from the assumption that a girl's role is to remain poised and attractive, regardless of what others say to her. I had to shatter the societal norms that dictate staying in a marriage for the sake of the children.

One of the most significant lies I have been told is that my happiness does not matter as much as the happiness of those around me. I was taught to put my desires aside and be a martyr to my children, partner, family members, school projects, volunteering, housekeeping, homemaking, and home cooking. I learned that at some point I had to choose between success in business and success at home.

What confined me was my acceptance of the lie that I could *not* have it all. A fulfilling career and wonderful children. A supportive husband who was also my best friend and partner. A life that contained both achievement and relaxation.

I created a life based on what I thought I was supposed to do rather than from my own heart's desire. I tried to fulfill everyone's expectations every single day, and no matter what I did, I felt that I was not good enough and that something was missing.

In my journey as a mother, part of me was drawn to pursuing my dreams and leveraging my talents. Another part of me wished to be involved in all my children's activities, as my own stay-at-home mom was with me. Each new role had its own compromises, sacrifices, and choices. I chose to sacrifice the stability of a corporate job in exchange for the flexibility I craved for my family. Embracing entrepreneurship enabled me to harmonize my worlds. I found a balance that worked for me.

I loved my work, and life was running like a well-oiled machine. The erosion of Self happened so slowly that I did not realize that I had lost myself. My concessions were small at first, neither deliberate nor conscious. Then, concession after concession, year upon year, I found myself in unfamiliar territory, much like a ship that had veered a mere degree off course overnight and then found itself hundreds of miles from its intended destination by dawn.

When we sacrifice our true self for a role, we do not know who we are when that role is stripped away. Think of the empty nester whose children have left the house, and the still-successful businessman who is forced to retire. Loss of a defining role can trigger feelings of uncertainty, loss of purpose, and a shift in perceived self-identity.

If I asked you to release yourself from your job titles, work, family roles, and everything you know yourself to be, who would you be? How would you describe yourself? What would you do? Are you doing it? If not, what is stopping you?

If something *is* stopping you, ask yourself, is it a self-imposed expectation? Or did you accept someone else's expectations?

When I became a mom, I subconsciously (and somewhat consciously) made a list of what it would take to be a great mom. On the days when my scorecard came up short, I knew I was a *Bad Mom* and could feel my kids' disappointment in me. I recall a particular day when I had forgotten something and started to apologize profusely to my seven-year-old son. In response, he gazed at me and lovingly said, "Mom, it's alright. You did your best. We all make mistakes." At that moment, I realized that the "bad mom" was only in my head.

When I assumed my roles of daughter, sister, friend, wife, and parent, no one handed me a rulebook telling me how to succeed. Yet somehow I placed expectations on myself and then held myself accountable to them. I created my own glass jars and then forgot I was the one who had screwed on the lids.

What I've come to understand is that I am the originator of the standards that define what it means to be a successful entrepreneur, partner, mother, daughter, and friend. I am the architect of those expectations, the one who sets the benchmarks, and the critic who beats myself up whenever I fall short.

With the invention of social media, it is easy to put your glass jar on a shelf to show it off, inviting both judgment and admiration. Carefully choreographed posts, filtered photos, humble brags, and exaggerated success stories paint the picture of the world we wish we lived in. They do not show the one that actually exists.

I recall when I discarded the notion of capturing the "perfect shot." I shared an Easter photo that featured my one-year-old playfully crawling away from her siblings, refusing to conform to sitting still and posing flawlessly. The memory still brings a smile to my face as it reflects the true essence of life. Those genuine moments hold the utmost significance—the grins beneath the Christmas tree, the cake-covered faces, the messy hair. It's not about the meticulously orchestrated snapshot on the way to church or the carefully chosen summer photo posted under the banner of "Merry Christmas" because it was the best family photo. I crave authenticity, the rawness of life, the depth of love.

What I've come to realize is that, frequently, those who appear to be the most dynamic on social media are often the ones who experience the deepest sense of invisibility. They put in significant energy to keep up appearances and show off how they excel in their expected roles. Yet, beneath the surface, they are struggling, running themselves ragged, and trying to convince *themselves* of the success that they are achieving and the quality of their life. Social media post popularity can increase insecurities or create a false sense of happiness.

I have always felt a strong inclination and pressure to achieve perfection. However, I have gradually come to understand that the pursuit of simultaneously excelling in all aspects of life is an unattainable goal. Life demands an ongoing equilibrium among its various parts. I concentrate on one facet, bring it into alignment, and then another aspect demands my attention. This cycle perpetuates itself, as alignment in one arena often throws a spotlight on another. When I embraced this pattern as the nature of life, everything instantly felt manageable.

I love this quote from an unknown author: "Don't be afraid of losing people. Be afraid of losing yourself by trying to please everyone around you." Prioritizing yourself doesn't mean letting people down or walking away. It just means being kinder to yourself. Loving yourself enough to stop and rest. Being brave enough to walk away.

If you encounter someone who is not supportive of your journey, recognize that they may not be the right match for your path—at least for now. Your true companions will delight in witnessing your inner fire rekindled. They will understand that you already have enough voices in your head and do not need their opinions. Instead, they will provide a safe haven filled with love, compassion, support, and encouragement.

As I began to reveal and express my genuine, unfiltered emotions—my sadness, pain, anger, and all the messy feelings in between—I rediscovered myself. As I began engaging in activities that brought me joy, my inner spark ignited, and my light shone brightly once more.

If you are ready to open your glass jar and reignite your spark, start saying yes to things that excite you and no to things that don't. It is time to dust off old hobbies and relearn how to play without inhibitions. It is time to step out of the constraints you have put on yourself and redefine what it is to be you. Fill your soul with passion, love with all your heart, and rediscover your spark.

Rachel Boone is a proud mother of four, accomplished entrepreneur, and experienced consultant with an unwavering commitment to fostering growth and transformation. Rachel leverages motivational guidance and strategic expertise to empower business owners across the United States, facilitating mindful business and marketing decisions aligned with their unique goals and personality. Rachel's entrepreneurial journey began in 2009 with TriLeaf Designs, and in 2016 she launched Rachel Boone Consulting. Transitioning in 2023, Rachel evolved TriLeaf Designs into Mindful Marketing and laid the groundwork for Sparked—a transformative collaboration of expertise for business owners. Educated with a BFA in Graphic Design, Certificate in Web Programming, and Executive MBA from Washington University in St. Louis, Missouri, Rachel values continuous personal and professional development. Beyond her endeavors, she actively engages in her community as a Cub Scout Leader, Chairman of the St. Louis Young Ambassadors, and Trail Adaptor for the Ozark Trail Association.

Rose Perry

Light Is Coming

Alone in my makeshift bedroom, which was truly a garage, I sat on my bed and contemplated the letter I had just written. Tears ran down my face as I picked up my journal to reread my last letter to the world. It stated, "I have tried being alive, and it is too hard. I can't take the pain anymore. It is better this way. To my family, I love you. I forgive you. And to the world, I hate you. Why didn't you see me?"

As I reread the letter, my mind raced with images of a childhood filled with poverty, abuse, and neglect. Insecurity and fear rang louder than a bell that night. Although I had begun attending church, the emotional and mental struggles I sought to resolve there had only intensified. I had fallen into a deep depression, and that night the room was filled with the cry of a girl who had given up.

As I held my journal open, I looked around for a razor blade to end the pain. Cutting myself was my only control in a life of chaos. The world didn't know it, but I had been struggling with suicide ideation and self-harm for a year. At this moment, I longed for the pain of the blade to numb the greater pain of my heartache. I had learned to like the stinging of the "healing" cuts. The pain gave me a kind of hope: that if the cuts on my wrist could heal, maybe the vast brokenness inside me could be healed as well.

Although this practice was familiar to me, the usual pattern was overshadowed by the very different plans I had made for that night. This time, things would be different. This time, I planned to cut as deep as I could until I bled to death. I took the razor blade and dug into my wrist, causing pools of blood to drip onto the journal that held my last words. Blinded by pain, tears, and anger, I watched the room around me grow dim. I slowly curled into a fetal position, waiting for my world to stop.

In what I thought would be my last moments, a tiny messenger came crawling into my room. Fear and confusion filled my mind as I watched my one-year-old niece make her way down the steps and into the dimly lit area. Although I felt too weak to move, concern that I was about to traumatize my niece provided motivation to sit up.

However, my niece seemed unfazed and on a mission. With pencil in hand, she crawled onto my lap and stared deep into my eyes. I was convinced that, at just one year of age, she had no concept of what was happening…until she found my bloody wrist. With the innocence of a child, she began to "erase" the blood with that end of her pencil. In that moment, the Holy Spirit spoke to me and said, "Rose, your hands were meant to serve me, not to harm my creation. You are my masterpiece."

Perhaps I just hadn't cut deeply enough, or maybe I overestimated the power of the blade, but I am sure about one thing: God was present with me that night in that garage. Not only did He stop my wrist from bleeding but He also sent my niece as a messenger to deliver a word that saved my life. I believe that my attempt should have been a death-defining moment. However, in that darkest of times, Christ loved me (Romans 5:8). He spoke life into my soul and filled me with the strength to live again. He filled me with hope and a future.

After my suicide attempt, God gave me the courage to share with the church leaders in my life what I was going through. Moved with compassion by what they heard, a couple that I was close to sought the Lord about how to help me. With much consideration and prayer, they adopted me and welcomed me into their family. My world changed overnight. It seemed as if all my prayers for a safe belonging had been answered. My world was falling into place.

However, even amidst relief and excitement, the emotional chaos and brokenness inside remained prevalent. Although I found myself safe, stable, and taken care of, I fought manic depression, night terrors, fear, and anxiety. There were weeks when I would cry myself to sleep every night, not even able to dress myself for bed. My adoptive mother would remove my shoes, place a blanket over me, and sing the Holy Spirit's sweet melody over me until I fell asleep. With a kiss on the forehead and a prayer sent to God, pieces of my brokenness were healing slowly.

I settled into a routine with my new family, and my relationship with God grew significantly. I attended a private Christian academy and allowed the institution, my church leaders, and God's Word to shape me into a young woman of God. In my late teens, I found myself dreaming, hoping, and wishing for more out of life than what I had been exposed to. God began to give me the desire to pursue higher education, to become a wife and a mom, and to be in full-time ministry. In obedience, I stepped out in faith and attended a two-year leadership college where God radically transformed my life.

During my first year of college, I awoke to the harsh reality that I still had a tremendous amount of pain and trauma to work through. I felt and performed differently from those around me. Where others were confident, I walked in insecurity. Where others were filled with power and strength, I felt weak and desperate for a touch from God. Where others were consistent and steady, I was emotionally unstable and undependable. I came across as bubbly, energetic, hopeful, and full of the Word of

God…but I still needed recognition that the wounded child in me was screaming for help. She simply wanted to be seen.

What I thought would end in ruin and failure transformed into the most impressionable season of growth in my life. I was surrounded by supportive leadership and caring friends who exposed my brokenness and led me to Christ. I began counseling, sought mentorship, and pressed into my relationship with God. Through a series of encounters with Christ, my heart continued to heal. Night terrors and pain from abuse were removed from my life. The darkness that once engulfed me shifted into marvelous light. Each time the enemy tried to use a life moment to define me as my pain, God reclaimed that moment, restoring and refining me for the purposes of His kingdom.

During that season of growth, the Lord asked me to find the meaning of my birth name: Ro'zhante. I grew weary of searching, but the Lord persisted that my name had a meaning. After searching through every English dictionary and failing, I stumbled upon a Persian dictionary. It was revealed that my name is Middle Eastern, specifically Kurdish Persian. It derives from Islamic origins. The first part, ROZHAN, means "day or light," and the second part, TÊ, means "is coming." With this discovery, I translated my name to "day/light is coming," and I finally understood much more than the meaning of my name.

From birth, God had a purpose and a plan for my life. Before I was born, I was given the promise of *His* light. Through every dark moment that I experienced, God was present, promising me that His light was coming, that I would see tomorrow, and that I was never alone. My name serves as a reminder that life will bring you dark moments, but Christ speaks a better Word. He is the restorer of all broken things.

If I could go back and tell the hurting girl anything, there are so many beautiful stories that I would share with her. For her future life is beautiful, godly, and full of laughter. Her world is graced with precious community, family, friends, ministry, and so much more. I would tell her, "There are many formative lessons ahead for you, dear girl. There are many people to love, and you have so much love to give."

Today I live many roles, such as daughter, girlfriend, sister, minister, graduate, friend, author, and communicator. With these labels comes pressure, responsibility, and honor. When I feel as though the crushing weight of expectation is too heavy and that I am not measuring up, I remind myself of the years of counseling, the hours spent in prayer on my face before the Lord, and the countless times I've sought wisdom, direction, and healing for my life. And, again, I am encouraged by the Lord.

My healing journey in life has been long and hard, but I find rest and hope in this simple truth: with each step of growth, healing, progress, and acceptance, a new life arrives. Like a butterfly, I am becoming a new creation. Like clay on the potter's wheel, I am being molded. With each new turning of a page in my book of life—each scratch, bruise, scar, and pain—I am reminded that I don't have to be perfect to make a difference. I don't have to be completely put together to allow others to read my book and become encouraged. In my vulnerability, those who feel unseen could feel seen. The hopeless could find hope.

Whether you are in your best season or worst season, God can show up and bring light and love into your situation. I stand in awe of a mighty God who saved me…and who continues to save me every day, every hour, every second. I have found a refuge in Him, and you can too.

Rose Perry is a strategist, communicating resources of hope. Her current role entails working alongside first-time guests to connect them to the church. She is a communicator, a minister, and a disciple of Christ. Her story is powerful and has impacted thousands at women's conferences and adoption agencies. Rose's number one goal is to see lives be radically transformed by the love of Jesus, as she practices being a witness. Rose graduated in 2018 from James River College with a degree in Leadership. She then attended Evangel University, where she earned a second degree in Behavioral Health: Mental Health Counseling. According to those nearest and dearest to her, Rose is best known for her outgoing personality, uplifting smile, and heart for Christ. Rose lives to tell the world that no matter how dark the night appears, light is coming.

Sara Chandler

The Grace Period

Extraordinary challenges…I've been through many in my life. Divorced parents in a world where parents didn't get divorced. Having many step-dads and a few stepmoms. Coping with attending sixteen different schools, all in the same county, trying to figure out whether I am the sports kid or the arts kid. What I did figure out was that I was the bisexual kid, and in the 1990s I thought it would be a great idea to come out in middle school. Yeah, no. Wrong idea, which caused the bullies to come out. And one more challenge: discovering in high school that one parent suffered from mental illness while the other one suffered from alcoholism.

My father set the bar for me: it was time to get an apartment because that is just what you do at eighteen. So I did, financing the expense with three jobs and friends to move in with; that was when my life changed. I thought I knew everything. I thought, "It isn't that hard to be out on your own; I have money."

Boy, was I wrong. I was evicted five months later because of a party my roommates threw while I was on vacation. That eviction and the credit record that followed me for seven years left me a full-time couch surfer from 2005 to 2015. During this time, I was so scared. I thought having the right job and the right car would get me anywhere. Well, I could eat, but where was I going to sleep? Where was I going to take showers? I couldn't go to work smelling dirty; I mostly worked with food.

I tried staying with some family members, but my work schedule meant coming and going at all hours, a nuisance to them. So I landed in romantic relationships and friendships that were not healthy, just to have a roof over my head. I worked multiple jobs, finding people here and there to stay with. I stayed in hotels with friends, and in my car a couple of times.

Turning to local assistance agencies, I learned I didn't qualify for help with housing because I earned too much, didn't have kids, or wasn't escaping a domestic violence situation. That was when a return to the couch-surfing lifestyle brought with it a drug problem. For two years I repeatedly put myself at risk for a place to sleep, and to have people around who didn't judge me for my situation. After I got clean, I realized that they didn't judge me, because the drugs helped us *all* not judge *anyone*. I was the only one with a job, so to them I looked great. But I wasn't. I didn't know who I was or where I was in life.

I was lost, racing between multiple jobs, putting myself in situations that made my life more complicated, and for what? To be in a relationship that made me cry literally every day, rather than be homeless? I didn't want to feel this pain anymore. I lost my best friend to a terrible disease, just short of a year after my grandfather passed away. Losing these two people left me with survivor's guilt and also a load of self-judgment, and I felt more alone than I'd ever thought possible. I wanted to leave this life of drugs and homelessness, and I prayed for my life to have purpose and meaning. I needed to change, to chase away some hard demons and go back to the root of things.

See, I had parents who worked very hard to feed me, clothe me, and clean me. But they didn't teach me about the expenses of being an adult, to *keep* that roof over my head and food coming in. They didn't know how to teach me relationship skills, mental health, budgets, investments, physical self-care. They could only teach me what they knew, and that was to survive and work for what you wanted. I learned job skills, how to respect others, and how to have money in my pocket, but not how to fix my car if it broke down or save money by cooking, rather than eating out. I was taught you work forty hours a week and get that paycheck. My father did everything he could to make me the person I am today, and I am proud to be that person; I just wish it hadn't been as hard as it was.

I had to teach myself these adult-living skills, not just for survival but for self-sufficiency. After I lost a friend to drugs, it wasn't hard for me to quit. Once clean, I realized how many other people I had "lost" because of my drug use. The couch to sleep on clearly wasn't worth the shadow side of this lifestyle. The withdrawal wasn't the worst part of getting sober; it was the mental, emotional, and physical pain of realizing what I had put myself through.

The hardest part was accepting responsibility for all I had lost: friends, family, support, my true self. Without drugs to numb them, difficult thoughts and emotions returned even stronger than before. Within two years of losing my best friend and grandfather, I was off drugs with no relapses and saving for my own place to live.

People ask me all the time how I do what I do. With so many challenges in my life, how do I still carry a smile on my face and music in my soul? Today, I run a nonprofit where I help the working homeless population move out of homelessness and into a self-sufficient life, through seven dimensions of well-being. At The Grace Period transitional housing, we offer financial empowerment and a mindset for success. I want to help those who, like me, just had some bad hands dealt to them and want to make their lives better. How do I do this? *Grace!*

I had to give myself grace to be the person I wanted to be, to realize that though I made decisions that resulted in homelessness and addiction, I couldn't keep blaming myself. I couldn't hide from my survivor guilt or the pain that the drugs suppressed, nor keep going from couch to couch just to feel the pride of not needing to ask my family for help.

Grace…I had to remember that I am a person and that God put me through this so I could survive, thrive, and be there for others like me. There is a meaning and purpose to everyone's life, and mine is to show people the same grace I show myself every day. "Giving yourself grace means making the choice to interact with the world—and yourself—with goodwill and kindness" (INTEGRIS Health, 2023). I had to be kind to myself, not beat myself up because I lived and they didn't. I stopped blaming myself for the shame my family felt about my lifestyle.

My family was always there for me when I let them know what was going on in my life. I lived in and out of my grandparents' house in my early twenties and stayed with my dad in my early thirties. What I have blamed myself for are all the times I didn't tell them about my problems—not trusting the family who cared about me more than the other people I chose during those dark times. I have done things that I'm not proud of to survive, things that I am still not yet ready to talk about, but I know that today I am a different person. I have a support system I didn't know I had.

I didn't deserve the abuse from the people I lived with as the price for a roof over my head. Though I wasn't consciously using them—I really did think I wanted those relationships—I can admit that I stayed longer than I should have. I went through relationships of physical abuse, mental abuse, infidelity, and even theft when I didn't think I had anywhere to go.

I had to remember that I am here for a reason, and I do have a purpose. I had to remember that my best friend and grandfather are looking down on me every day to cheer me on and build me into this woman of grace and capability, to do what I am meant to do.

Anyone can go into their version of survivor mode; anyone can do what they need to, to get the job done. And, also, anyone can make themselves complete. My lesson is that, if I am not kind to myself from the grace inside me, then how can I expect anyone else to show me kindness? Now I know who I am, live how I want to live, enjoy the time I have, and rejoice in all I receive. As I do all that, I remember to breathe the word "grace" and allow myself to see my purpose and the meaning of my life.

Reference

INTEGRIS Health. What Does Giving Yourself Grace Mean? Taken from www.integrisok.com on September 31, 2023.

Perfectly I'Mperfect

Sara Chandler is the executive and cofounder of The Grace Period transitional housing program, supporting the working homeless in St. Charles County. The Grace Period helps community members regain self-sufficiency after a time they did not plan for. After starting as a cook at the local bowling alley at age fourteen, Sara pursued a culinary career, including classes at Le Cordon Bleu. After retiring from the hospitality industry, Sara founded The Grace Period transitional house in 2019 as a 501(c)(3) nonprofit. So far, the program has six graduates and has helped twenty-five other families with resources to regain self-sufficiency. In her free time, Sara enjoys singing, spending time with her family, and making time for herself in the quiet, giving her the space and grace she needs.

Sarah Lowe

Plan B

I was in my early twenties. I had just landed a full-time teaching position in the grade level I really wanted at an elementary school in my hometown. I'd found an amazing apartment in a historic building with people I knew living on each of the other three floors and was in a relationship that was going well. It felt like I was living the life I was supposed to be. Until, one day, I noticed something very strange.

My left arm and hand felt numb and tingly…like I'd been lying on them for too long and they'd fallen asleep. What made this strange was the fact that I hadn't been lying on them at all. And they weren't waking up. After a couple of days, my coworkers convinced me to go see a doctor. They said I'd probably just pinched a nerve. Something simple. I mean, what else could it be?

Within the first twenty minutes of that appointment, the doctor said he suspected I might have multiple sclerosis, but he wasn't qualified to make that kind of diagnosis. He referred me to a neurologist, who, suspecting the same, ordered a series of tests including an MRI of the brain.

Like a lot of people, I am terrified of needles. So when I learned they would need to inject a contrast dye during the procedure, I panicked. The technician said she could make a note that I refused the dye *unless* she noticed something during the first half of the test. Then, she said, she would have to go ahead with the injection. So when the machine stopped its rumbling and banging and she came back into the room with a needle in her hand, I realized something might actually be wrong. And when the neurologist called to schedule the appointment to discuss the results—and suggested that I bring a family member or friend with me—I knew.

Something was definitely wrong.

The MRI gave us four possible diagnoses to consider. The visible mass on my brain that I was now seeing for myself could have been the result of a brain tumor, a brain infection, multiple sclerosis, or a stroke. I remember how my head was spinning as I looked at the image and reality began to sink in. I didn't even know which diagnosis to hope for. But after a few weeks and several more tests, I was diagnosed with MS.

Once my family, friends, and coworkers learned of my diagnosis, I was regularly greeted with "Hey. How are you doing?" complete with a furrowed brow and nodding head tilt. I was also treated to stories about others' family, friends, and neighbors—and even the occasional "woman at my church," all of whom had MS and most of whom eventually found themselves visually impaired, unable to speak clearly, in a wheelchair, and/or walking with a cane. Those stories were not very comforting, but I'm sure everyone meant well. So many of us just don't know what to say to somebody in a case like this.

Coming to terms with the very real possibility that at least one of those stories would eventually be mine, I accepted the fact that I would just have to manage the best that I could—both mentally and physically. And as this particularly difficult chapter in my life continued to unfold, I was grateful to have found a neurologist who I liked and trusted, and I was getting some much-needed support from my family and friends.

And I was doing OK…for a while anyway.

Sarah Lowe | Plan B

As I mentioned before, I was a second-grade teacher—and really good at it too. So when my MS symptoms started flaring up more frequently and began jeopardizing my work, it was time to consider one of the few drug treatments available for MS patients at that time. My boyfriend had to give me an intramuscular injection every Sunday. It was awful. The medication gave me body aches, chills, and a headache that lasted for two or three days, so I started off every single work week struggling to teach effectively despite the aggravating side effects. Those injections single-handedly ruined my Sundays and probably my relationship. But I didn't stop taking them…even though I wanted to. I knew they were necessary to keep my symptoms in check well enough for me to continue teaching.

After a while, though, despite the regular injections, my symptom flare-ups were becoming increasingly significant. One evening while playing cards with friends, I realized that I couldn't shuffle the deck and had to ask for help. Another night, I couldn't carry two drinks from the bar to our table because my left hand couldn't even grasp one. It wasn't long before I had completely lost the use of my left hand. I couldn't feel it or use it—at all.

Because I'm left-handed, I had to learn to do a lot of things differently. I graded papers and paid bills writing with my right hand, wore mittens instead of gloves, bought some easy-to-fasten belts because I couldn't button my pants, and stopped wearing jewelry altogether. My boyfriend had to fasten my coat for me, and a coworker would button the right cuff of my shirt when I got to work. It wasn't easy, but I was getting through it. I was adapting. I was doing OK.

Or so I thought.

Then one day, I decided to make a bologna sandwich, and I wanted some mayonnaise on my sandwich. But no matter what I did or how hard

I tried, I could not get the lid off of the jar. And *that* was the proverbial straw that broke the camel's back. I sank onto the tile floor in front of my refrigerator and cried until I couldn't breathe. After everything else I had withstood up to this point, I completely lost it over a teaspoon of mayonnaise on a bologna sandwich.

Of course, I did eventually get up off the floor. It took three months, but the feeling in my arm and hand gradually came back, and I was ready for life to get back to normal. What I didn't know, however, was that "normal" life for me would now include things like the temporary loss of color vision in my left eye, patches of skin that itch so intensely I have to wear socks on my hands when I sleep so I won't wake up bleeding, and feeling like the skin on my stomach is three inches thick. Bouts of fatigue are still so bad that it's a struggle just to get out of bed. My limbs feel so heavy that it's like I'm wearing a weighted blanket all day. At one point, I even started walking with a cane.

I fought as hard as I could, for as long as I could, to continue teaching. With help from my administration, I was able to work a modified work week. I would teach Mondays, Wednesdays, and Fridays while the same substitute teacher covered Tuesdays and Thursdays. That helped for a while, but eventually I had to accept the fact that teaching is not a part-time job. My MS was affecting my work, and my work was affecting my MS.

I have always been a doer—always busy, always thinking, always planning, always working. The decision to stop teaching and go on disability was a tough one. My neurologist once told me that there are two Sarahs. There's the old Sarah who was always busy, active, hard-working, and energetic; and there is a new Sarah who can't do what the old Sarah used to do. I needed to accept this new Sarah and did the hardest thing I will ever have to do—quit teaching.

I left my twenty-five-year teaching career with a hundred and fifty unused sick days that *had* to be used before I could receive disability benefits or take a part-time job. Between being unable to work and the world going into quarantine, I was desperate to find validation and purpose. Then I found out that some friends of mine whose regular jobs had been put on hold were rewriting their future too. They were taking a leap of faith and opening a record store. They were set to open the store right about the time I would be permitted to work, so I reached out to them about working there for just a few hours a week, and they accepted! It was the epitome of a match made in heaven. I feel so blessed to have worked there for more than two-and-a-half years now, and I'm pretty sure they are feeling blessed too.

In addition to having MS, I have struggled with anxiety and depression for many years. I was also diagnosed with skin cancer just over a year ago and will continue to have biopsies and surgeries to remove the cancerous cells every two or three weeks—until they have found and removed all existing cancer and no new cancers come to the surface.

Life can be very hard and is consistently unpredictable. There will be struggles. Ten or twenty years ago, I would never have imagined working part time at a record store at age fifty-three, but here I am. Even though I am no longer able to teach, I have come to realize that validation and purpose can be found almost anywhere. You don't have to do big things. Just be willing to do as much as you can, when you can. Only then can you discover a new purpose and begin to thrive again.

Sarah Lowe taught elementary school for twenty-five years in what she considered the ideal setting. A unique approach and flair for the creative showed Sarah's students firsthand that you don't have to fit into a common mold to be successful and happy. This advocacy for being "not like the others" carries into her personal life as well. Sarah's love of music, nostalgia, children's literature, toys, and collectibles can be seen throughout her home. Every room and even the hallway are brimming with toys, lunch boxes, record players, holiday decorations, and more. If it makes Sarah smile, it's on display. Writing has always been a fulfilling creative outlet for Sarah. She began writing poems and stories when she was just seven years old—and hasn't stopped writing ever since. She is both excited and privileged to share just one of her stories with you, here, in *Perfectly I'Mperfect*.

Shashanna Davis

Sisu

(SEE-soo)

I wearily stepped onto the bathroom's cold tile floor, exhausted and drained from the night before. As I turned on the shower, I was flooded with the memories of each time my husband had laid his hands on me throughout our marriage. I slowly stepped under the warm water and began to cry. A gut-wrenching silent cry, like the center of my soul was being ripped out of me. I ugly cried in silence for what seemed like forever and begged God for the strength to do what I needed to do.

I had threatened to leave him for years. We even spent a year separated before the birth of our third child. But after the prior night's look of rage and darkness in his eyes, like that of someone with no soul, as he held our three-month-old baby girl and spoke to our son through gritted teeth practically foaming at the mouth…I was done.

I knew that leaving would be harder than staying. Staying was a learned skill. I knew what buttons to push or not, what eggshells to tiptoe around, what to say, and when it was OK to say it. Leaving…well, leaving was going to be a whole new experience. Leaving was something not yet fully experienced. The unknown was far scarier than staying, but after twelve years of this known fear, I was through.

Sisu allowed me to do what I knew in my heart must be done. There is no direct English translation for this Finnish word—the extraordinary and indomitable spirit required to go beyond limitations in the face of adversity. Friends over the years have seen in me an inner strength that not many others possess. Some have even told me I am an inspiration to them. Sisu is what I think they saw in me, and sisu got me through one of the hardest seasons of my life.

I hadn't gotten much sleep the night before, but I knew what I had to do. It was now or never; I could no longer continue to live like this. I would no longer allow my son to believe that this is the way a man should treat a woman, and I would not let my daughters believe that they had to accept this type of treatment.

I can't say that at that moment I fully believed that I deserved better, but I knew without a doubt I was done. I was tired of settling, and if by chance he was right that no one else would ever want me, I was OK with being alone. When I heard myself tell my husband that I would rather deal with our children's broken hearts from his death than continue to deal with him any longer, I knew this relationship had to be over. I had clung on to the all-important two-parent household aspiration for so long because neither my husband nor I had that growing up. Finally, I realized two happy homes would be better than one miserable one.

Out of the shower, getting dressed, I started slamming doors and cabinet drawers. I flicked lights on as he continued to sleep on the couch. I pounded my heels into the floors, obnoxiously doing all I could to agitate him. I needed a reason to leave. So I picked a fight. It didn't take long for a full-on World War III to ensue, complete with police, who eventually took him off to jail.

I went immediately into autopilot. I got the kids ready for school and dropped them off. I went to work and, for the first time, shared with my

Shashanna Davis | Sisu (SEE-soo)

boss and coworkers what I had been living with. This telling of the secret was a huge step because I had essentially been living a double life. Until then, only one person in the office had any clue to my secret, and she kept it guarded, helping me when she could.

My husband would eventually spend five months in the State of California prison system. Meanwhile, I raised our three children and continued school to complete my bachelor's degree with the help of my in-laws. As I traveled extensively for work, I wrote my papers on airplanes or in hotel rooms. I went to baseball and cheer practices on the evenings I was home and on the weekends. When my husband was released, the kids and I were in our own apartment trying to make a new normal.

When reality set in for him, that our former home was not there to receive him, things became heated again: phone calls, threats, showing up in my office begging to talk, begging for one more chance, and promising this time it would be different. I did not waver; I was through.

Six months after leaving him, I filed for divorce. Shortly after, I received the call that my mom was in the hospital back in Missouri and I needed to come home right away. It was a whirlwind of a trip; I arrived on Wednesday, and by Friday I was having to make the decision to end life-saving efforts. I once again felt that gut-wrenching agony pulling my soul out of my body. My mother taught me many things in life, but she hadn't taught me how to live in a world where she didn't exist. In fact, growing up an only child with a single mom, at times we felt more like sisters.

Suddenly, at thirty, I found myself motherless, fatherless, an only child, and a single mom of three kids. Some who knew me were afraid that, after my mother's death, I would go back my husband. While it sometimes seemed like the easier option, I did not. I can honestly say that if it weren't for my youngest child, I could have allowed myself to fall apart. The older two could make a sandwich and pour some cereal, but my baby needed me, so I couldn't break. With the support of two of my best friends, his parents, and sisu, I persevered.

I spent the next half year grieving the loss of my mother, finishing school, and trying to choose the best path forward for the kids and me. For the first few months after my mom's death, I spent hours on the phone with my friend back in Missouri. I cried, I yelled, I was angry, I was afraid, but I slowly gained my strength.

As I was finishing classes for my bachelor's degree, I was no longer getting monetary support from my ex-husband. I began contemplating moving back to Missouri for a lower cost of living and agonized for months about uprooting the kids from the only state they'd ever lived in. Was it the right thing to move back to a place where my mom no longer was? I put challenges or ultimatums in front of God: *If this is the right decision, then this needs to happen or fall into place.* God continued to deliver, and I continued to doubt and question all the requested signs as I received them because they weren't blatant *turn-here-dummy* signs.

Following months of consideration and conferring and justifying my decision to those who cared, I made the decision to move back to Missouri. My in-laws tried to get me to stay. They even offered to pay for the baby's child care and let us live with them. But…sisu…I knew I needed to stand on my own two feet, and I knew that in Missouri I could do that.

After nine years of living in California, I returned to my home state and started healing. It has been a long, slow process with a lot of doubt all along the way about whether I made the right decision. Recovering from trauma is a process. While the physical bruises heal and disappear quickly, the mental recovery can take years.

Life can sometimes pile obstacles on you, making you feel like you can't go on. Persevering despite the feeling you want to give up is a personal strength. Sisu—that extraordinary and indomitable spirit—allows you to reach deep inside and muster the strength and perseverance to do what must be done. So when you don't see a way out or don't believe you are strong enough to do it, call upon your sisu. Where do you need it right now?

Shashanna Davis is a mid-level manager in manufacturing, with her MBA, who is also an independent sales consultant with Norwex and Scentsy. Happily remarried now, she loves, likes, and accepts herself, no longer settling for less than she deserves. Her two older children have graduated high school and started their adult lives, while her "baby" is still home, finishing high school.

Shelly Clark

Wins Aren't Always Determined by a Score

Six years ago, when my life was in a state of chaos, a unique opportunity presented itself. It took this small-business owner out of her comfort zone and threw her into the arena—literally an arena—as the majority owner of a men's professional indoor soccer team.

In 2003, my husband Will and I started our land surveying business with our knowledge and experience and a $2,500 tax return. We purchased used equipment and pounded the pavement searching for clientele. We worked out of the kitchen of our mobile home, drove our small sedan to job sites, and worked harder than I thought I was capable of. Three years later, we were so busy that Will quit his full-time job and we hired our first employee. Our company's mission has always been to produce accurate results with exceptional service. Twenty years later, our five-star ratings on Google, Facebook, and Angi, and an A+ rating by the Better Business Bureau, testify that we've upheld that mission.

Ten years into our journey we realized we needed to start thinking outside the box and decided to sponsor a local professional indoor sports team. We used this opportunity to get to know our clients on a personal level and to create friendships with them by inviting them to games. As the saying goes, we do business with people we know, like, and trust. Our business grew by leaps and bounds over the next few years. I could not have predicted that our success would be the catapult of my personal destruction.

I'll spare you the drama and events leading up to the state of chaos, but twelve years in, some of the people who I considered my closest and best friends betrayed me. I was in a bad place, as I questioned my worth and value, questioned loyalty and trust. I tried to find answers, created justifications, made excuses. My self-confidence was destroyed, and I felt alone and lost.

At my personal low point, the opportunity presented itself to become the owner of that local sports team. Will and I were thriving with our surveying business, and I thought this could provide me with the opportunity I needed to redefine myself and rebuild my confidence. So we seized the opportunity and became majority owners of a men's professional indoor soccer team.

I suppose it's no surprise to hear that I jumped in with both feet, but I also had *no* idea what I was doing. I knew how to build a business, how to treat people with respect, and how to communicate. I thought I was smart enough—or at least my transcript said I should have been. I thought "surely this elementary school teacher who built a very successful business from the ground up could figure it out."

And so it started: a greater challenge than I expected. That first season I learned several hard lessons. The greatest of them was that social media is not kind. People who were friendly and supportive to my face became the polar opposite when they were in the comfort of their homes, able to be keyboard warriors, expecting that their criticism would have a positive impact.

Our team struggled and ended the season with one win and nineteen losses. Fans were upset, rightfully so, and were very vocal. They gave us credit for stepping up when no one else would and for buying the team to keep it from folding. They also provided unsolicited advice as to what to do, what changes to make, and how to spend our finances on the team to turn the it around.

This new opportunity was supposed to help me rebuild myself, rather than lead me to question my every move. I couldn't help but read through *all* the comments on every social media post someone made about the team, about me. As with my friends' betrayal, I began to question my value and self-confidence. I was letting others tear me down and influence me, my goals, and my vision for the team.

My husband urged me to quit reading, to quit caring about what others thought and wrote. That first season forced me to put on my big-girl pants, make difficult decisions, and define what my priorities were for the team. We had to reinvent ourselves and adapt our strategies to earn the fans' support. We enhanced our game-day experience and brought in a new coach to transition the mindset of the players. That next season we had three wins; the season after that, ten. I thought I had figured it out. I thought the negativity on social media was behind us. I thought the increase in wins, attendance, and experience was enough to keep our loyal fans engaged and satisfied.

I was wrong.

In March of 2023, the Major Arena Soccer League (MASL) published an article celebrating the fact that I was the first female owner in the league, which has professional teams across the nation and in Mexico. I was interviewed by Michael Lewis from the League, who wrote a lengthy article about me, the role that I currently play in the league, and my approach to running a team.

The MASL published the article, and it was shared across dozens of media channels. From my perception, it was a norm-breaking article as it spoke about how "winning" isn't always defined by the final score shown on the scoreboard, and how we can have other goals and focuses that can be just as important as the game's final score.

The article saw positive, encouraging engagement by fans and sponsors. However, a thread involving several "fans" on a social media fan page ridiculed me, saying I was in over my head. They argued that our team was "never going to succeed if the owner of the team doesn't value winning."

Initially, their words broke me. I'm not afraid to admit that those words took me back to six years before and made me question what I was doing and how I was doing it. I broke down in tears. However, unlike tears of the past, these cleared my vision, washed away the negativity, and left me laser-focused to speak up and stand strong for my philosophy that winning isn't limited to only the outcome on a scoreboard.

The article stated, "Like just about every sports team owner, Shelly Clark would love to win a championship or two" (Lewis, M., 2023). My very *first* statement in the interview was that I want our team to win a championship, which requires those scoreboard wins. The article then discussed how winning, to me, is also about the atmosphere, the experience, and the connections that are made by the people who "show up" and put their phones down.

Winning is the little girl catching a T-shirt and then high-fiving her dad; it's the group of kids trying to get on the video board by dancing with popcorn buckets on their heads; and it's a boy giving his grandpa a hug because his favorite player just scored! Those memorable, adrenaline-driven moments have tremendous value. They likely have a greater overall impact on our lives than a team winning a game.

My question is: Why do people think that the only way to win is to have a higher score than the opponent? Why don't we ever consider that winning is more than just competing against someone? Why be so narrow-minded? Why limit the joys in your life when there are so many opportunities? Why allow others to define what winning is to you?

For me, winning is about working collaboratively for the greater good. It's about having that unique experience, creating that memory that no one else can replicate or ever take away from you. It's those feelings of exuberance that you experience—that's the win! While I do also value the numbers on the scoreboard, that single outcome doesn't define my entire experience. My hope is that those who come to the games feel that exuberance and embrace my outlook.

I am still learning how to overcome public ridicule; I anticipate this is a lifelong lesson for most of us. What I have found invaluable is to clearly define what a "win" is and acknowledge that I alone am the author of that definition.

My definition is continually evolving, and I try to remember that I have the choice to *always win*. It's a win when I am able dismiss the chaos and work through challenges. It's a win to focus on the extraordinary moments and cherish the memories that I'm making. Winning is having the confidence to know that I am enough, that my thoughts and opinions are valid, and that I don't have to pretend to be someone I'm not.

And most importantly, because I know myself well enough to know that I'm going to read all those posts and comments on social media, that there's a difference between "hearing" and "listening." I hear all the comments, but now the win is that I only *listen* to those that are positive and build me up.

Life is short. Time is limited. Let's choose to win.

REFERENCE

Lewis, Michael. (March 4, 2023), "Shelly Clark: MASL's first female majority owner," online at https://www.maslsoccer.com.

Shelly Clark grew up in Ohio and graduated Magna Cum Laude from Kent State University in 1997 with a Bachelor's of Science in Education. In 2001 she and her husband Will moved to St. Charles, Missouri, starting Cardinal Surveying & Mapping in 2003. In 2013, the Clarks became minority owners of the St. Louis Ambush professional indoor soccer team, and then majority owners in 2016, just as Shelly earned her license as a professional land surveyor. Shelly currently serves as the CEO of the St. Louis Ambush, overseeing day-to-day operations, and serves as Treasurer on the Major Arena Soccer League Executive Committee. Shelly and Will are involved in their local community, serving and supporting several local charities, including Action for Autism, Youth in Need, Greater Giving, and many others. The Clarks have two grown children and reside in Cottleville, Missouri.

Tonya Steinmeyer and Keri Szwarc

All for a Reason

Pause and think about a time when you felt out of place, when something about you didn't suit or fit a situation. Maybe what rings a bell is the persistent and invasive questions of "what if" playing like a broken record in your head: What if my body was more feminine, I tried harder at my marriage, was thinner, give him one more chance to change, listened to my gut…Or perhaps a feeling of more general inadequacy sometimes plagues your mind. It may seem silly, but we invite you to, right now, close your eyes and feel whether any of these I-should-be-different thoughts or variations hit home for you.

Elements in our environment all play a part in our perception of ourselves and those around us. Some elements seem obvious, such as a commercial that shows life is better when you are thinner, or a TV show that portrays happy families as a man and woman with children. Some elements seem inconsequential, like a random comment from a family member or snide joke from a friend. Other times our perceptions stem from repeated actions of family members that tell us we are not good enough. Our experiences inform and affect how we see ourselves, in reference to the criteria society defines as success.

All these what-if questions and doubts plagued both of us as we lived lives our society labeled as successful. We both struggled with the sense that our lives were not what they should be, and yet could not readily define why we felt this way.

We each fought this lonely mental battle every day. And some days the mental struggle carried physical symptoms, such as lack of sleep, fatigue, exhaustion, short temperedness, lethargy, and hyper-awareness. Some days it manifested as a general unease, as if more than just one other shoe was waiting to drop.

Before we met, these mental and physical battles took their tolls on each of us. After we met, became friends, and started dating, we together accepted and embraced the thought that everything happens for a reason. Everything that happened to us before we met made us who we are now for each other, our children, and ourselves.

We remind each other often: everything happens for a reason. We each fought our own battles before we met five years ago, each arriving from a traditional marriage defined as one man plus one woman equals children. Each struggling as wives in marriages that felt not quite right, we made them work according to the societal norms we both accepted.

Grit, persistence, and the drive to be better versions of ourselves led us through all the obstacles and into each other's lives. We love and accept each other for all our quirky, stumbling, lovable, and frustrating traits. Each day, we support and challenge each other to not get hung up on being perfect, and to focus instead on being consistently present for ourselves, each other, and our family.

Tonya was married for twenty-four years to a man who, from all appearances, loved her, and she loved him. She took care of everything for their three children. She shuttled them to and from martial arts. She participated in the PTA and volunteered for school events. She took the boys on camping trips with her parents, while her husband stayed home and worked. In many ways, she was a single parent to her three boys.

Yet, with all that life moving all around her, Tonya never felt truly comfortable in her own body. It seemed to her that she was missing something…that feeling you get when something is not quite right, yet you lack the words to describe what is "off" or what is missing. That's what sat on Tonya's mind for most of that marriage. She tried all the *what ifs*: being more feminine by getting her nails done; altering her appearance in the hopes of erasing the sense that she was lacking something as a woman; dieting, thinking that if she weighed less, that sense of needing to be something *more* would be met. None of those alterations of self ever seemed to fill that sense of something missing or resolve that sense that something was not right.

She fought, as a mom should, when one of her children was constantly bullied for his choices in sexual orientation. She struggled and worked through the mental toll of the bullying on her child, and the ripple effects on her and her other children. She fought to protect him, encourage him, and understand him. She suffered because he suffered. Tonya chose to learn as much as possible regarding her son's choices. As she supported him, she also recognized something in herself, realizing that her "missing" element had absolutely nothing to do with her appearance.

Recognizing and accepting she had suppressed a key element of her true self, and working to help her son through his struggles, she found her true sexual orientation as a lesbian. Embracing this piece of herself meant honoring who she truly was, which brought the internal peace she had been searching for…but also brought the upheaval of divorce for her family. She chose that hard path anyway, to show her children that making hard choices to respect yourself is worth the effort and pain.

When Tonya met Keri, Keri was a year out from her traditional marriage, which had also looked perfect from the outside and yet had been far from that. Keri, too, felt the furthest thing from perfect as she struggled with the anxiety that if she did not do everything perfectly, her ex-husband would win custody of their children. Every choice she faced required an outcome that met the needs of her children. She fought the uphill battle to be perfect, as required to protect her children from their mentally abusive father.

Keri came to realize that to truly protect her boys and make sure they had what they needed, she must find who *she* was. She went back to yoga, finding comfort and reassurance in granting herself permission to be still. She went to the library and wandered aimlessly without worrying about being somewhere at a specific time. She created dance parties in the kitchen with her boys and her mom.

Keri laughed with her boys over silly things; she got down on the floor and played with them. She went for a walk without taking her cell phone. She sat outside reading while grilling dinner, played card games with the family, attended family functions, and participated in conversations. She enjoyed listening to any radio station she wanted. She accepted that all these "little" things are important and valuable parts that answer the question, "Who is Keri?"

She accepted friendship and encouragement from coworkers, learning she was more than just a survivor. She was a thriver. Keri grew personally, more and more, as she accepted in both her head and heart that she did not need to be perfect. Perfection was a myth she had bought into, one perpetuated by others to control her. Now, she chose to be messy and emotional, to laugh and be loud, to be quiet and observant. She made choices that made her happy, which meant her boys could be happy.

Seeing her boys happy and being able to grow beyond the four walls of a house was all she wanted. Throughout this transformation, Keri never anticipated finding someone outside of her birth family who loved *all* of her, all her quirks, anxieties, and habits. She did not plan on finding someone she could trust to love her children just as much as she did. She did not plan on finding anyone willing to take on the "work in progress" that she was and still is. She had not factored in that belief that everything happens for a reason.

Tonya and Keri became friends and then partners. Now, *they* are a "we."

And now we have what each always thought should exist in true marriage or partnership. Each of us is behind the other, to encourage and support each other to do what needs to be done, and to become the best versions of ourselves. We intentionally walk beside each other, as a constant reminder that neither is alone in her journey. When either of us reaches the point where she does not know how to move forward, the other takes the lead, helping clear the path or change the course if needed. Together, we share the gift of six amazing boys ranging from six to twenty-one years of age.

No day is perfect, because perfection is a myth. Rather than being perfect, our shared goal each day is to be present for each other and our boys. Every day offers some situation that challenges us to rethink how we approach a problem and what that means as a couple. Many of the challenges we face every day, we find, start in our minds, in our thoughts.

Some days our new form of perfection is accepting that neither of us can protect our children from being hurt by the actions of people who should love them unconditionally. Other days it means we fight old habits like pleasing others, or respect the boundaries of our children, or confront mental triggers that negatively impact our relationships with each other and our children. Daily obstacles require balancing the emotional needs of all six of our children and ourselves at the same time. The days when we find this balance are the days that fall into the category of being great. That outcome is worth working through the obstacles and challenges presented by our internal habits and external environment.

Everything that happened to us before we met happened for a reason. We would not be the individuals or couple we are today if our pasts had been different. Now well beyond that striving for false perfection, we both prefer to be *imperfectly perfect*. We choose to be *present* for each other and our children, rather than trying to live up to unrealistic expectations.

Tonya Steinmeyer and Keri Szwarc | All for a Reason

Tonya Steinmeyer and Keri Szwarc commit to and value a strong relationship rooted in trust and helping each other live their best lives. In their blended family, they are mothers to six unique and amazing boys ranging in age from six to twenty-one. They live west of St. Louis with their children, bearded dragon, and energetic dog. Tonya is developing skills in Neuro-Linguistic Programming to provide support and encouragement to the LGBTQ community and working toward her dream of buying, rehabbing, and renting homes. Keri enjoys interacting with and encouraging the individuals around her, snapping candid photos of her family, and cooking with all their kids.

Tracee White

No Isn't a Bad Word

At thirty-six, I found myself starting over after ending my thirteen-year marriage. I was scared but optimistic about my future. When I decided to divorce my husband, my focus was on my two children and how they would feel about our new normal. When people asked me how I was doing, my response was always, "I'm good."

That simple response put me in the category of "strong friend." At first, I didn't understand that role or the responsibility that comes with the label.

I was just twenty years old and already a mom when I met my husband, and was focused on financial stability for my one-year-old. I didn't invest in any of what I needed to grow and excel in life. By twenty-three, I was not only a mom but also a wife. Yet, even after the whole thirteen years with him, when the divorce hit, my focus was still on my kids, not me.

I remember a consultation with a therapist for my then sixteen-year-old son. As I explained to the therapist what was happening in our lives and why I felt my son needed therapy, he responded, "I actually think we need to focus on you first."

That was my normal: I suppressed my needs and desires, and put the needs of others first. Even when I went back to school during the marriage, my goal was to earn a degree that would allow me to contribute more to the household finances, rather than to pursue any of my passions and desires.

My mother was my blueprint for this phase of my life; she was also a young mother, just sixteen and unmarried when I was born. When I was eight, she married, and I fell in love with my stepdad. He simply became my daddy, and I wanted something similar for my son. My goal was to marry someone who worked as hard as my dad had, to have a partner who loved my child as much as he loved me. I wanted to create the life for my son that my mother created for me.

Like my mom, I was a young mother who grew up believing that providing for the family was the most important goal, not following personal passions. It was important for me to *provide* and to have a spouse with the same interests.

I didn't have many examples of entrepreneurship, and I was the first of my grandmother's grandchildren to graduate from college. I had never seen a person follow dreams or work toward their passions, so as a young mother I focused on ensuring that my child was taken care of, while subconsciously ignoring what I truly needed.

I never calculated for "what if it doesn't work out?" If I didn't know who I was at thirty-six and divorcing, there's no way I knew way back at twenty-three when marrying. Being aware of other possible outcomes would have meant attending to what was going on with me and my relationship with my husband. That kind of self-awareness had been so far down my priority list, I'd never gotten to it.

The first thing therapy taught me was to stop pouring from an empty cup, to give from my overflow. Those words are easy to say, but the reality is harder to live. I was a fixer, an enabler. I would see someone as broken and, if they told me they loved me, I would do anything necessary to fix them, despite all the evidence that they were clearly wrong for me.

Looking back, I can see my questionable relationship choices started at the age of eighteen. In therapy, I discovered deep-rooted and previously hidden issues with my biological father as some of the causes of these choices. I hid a lot of my younger missteps from my parents because I knew I was raised to know better.

But by eighteen years of age, I knew that I shouldn't allow someone I was dating to raise a hand to me, so I confided in a friend's stepdad. He was a dad, right? I knew I couldn't tell *my* stepdad, who loved me as deeply as any biological father would. He would expect me to end the relationship, and I knew I wasn't ready to do that. I finally did so, but that experience had already locked me into a lack of self-love and endless rounds of trying to fix others while I continued to break.

For a while after the divorce, I repeated this pattern while dating. However, with growing awareness, thanks to my therapist, I began to learn more about myself and my patterns. The journey wasn't easy, but we made good progress. We were *getting there*, but all was not "fixed" yet. Because I had learned how to build protective walls around my heart, at the first sign of any trouble I just ran. If my friends thought I was the strong friend before, now I became known as the no-BS friend. I didn't tolerate much…or so I thought.

For about five years, I remained in my normal pattern, still ignoring some red flags in hopes of being "chosen." I dated people I knew weren't for me, allowing the relationships to go on longer than needed, hoping for a breakthrough. Yet I was enduring breakup after breakup instead. Each time, I called my therapist and asked for a "re-up," seeing myself as a wounded bird that needed to be patched up yet again, and to figure out what I was not yet learning.

I had allowed myself to be broken every single year by someone new. After the fifth and final relationship, I decided to stop dating, to really focus on myself. Slowly, I learned to be aware of what I needed, and—when I did start dating again—I recognized the red flags I'd missed before and stopped ignoring the ones I'd been barely noticing. I began to realize I wouldn't miss out on anything if I let go of these unfulfilling relationships *sooner* rather than later.

From my perspective now, I can see that I learned at a young age to allow others to make me feel *less than*. I allowed them to validate whether I was worthy of love. And I continued doing that until I finally, truly felt self-love. I adopted the phrase "I'm perfectly imperfect" as a way to encourage and love on myself regardless of any flaws. I became the queen of the social media hashtag #self-love in my quest to identify boundaries. I came to understand that, when my cup is nearly empty, there is nothing I can pour out for others. I had to *believe* that it was OK before I could only pour for others from my overflow…before I even *produced* an overflow.

When I turned forty, I knew that I would never be that same timid girl who loved everyone else before she loved herself. I was discovering how it felt to pursue *my* passions, and what it meant to believe I could have my heart's desire. From this place of strength, I relaunched an old business that I had loved but put aside.

Now, I am willing to tell others no, and I no longer seek to make everyone else happy before making myself happy. I also have become a better mom, and in March of 2021 I met the man who is now my husband. I showed up exactly as I am, loving every part of me.

This journey of extraordinary overcoming hasn't been the easiest, but I can say honestly that I regret nothing about my past. Through every struggle, I learned, and those lessons helped me to become better than I was. We are developmental people, so I know the journey of learning isn't over. There's always more room to grow, and I embrace this in my perfectly imperfect life.

A licensed Zumba instructor for more than thirteen years, Tracee is a champion for wellness. In 2020, she rebranded and relaunched her luxury home fragrance collection as MLCA Lux Aura, to champion spiritual and mental health, as well as physical. She motivates and uplifts others as a certified life coach dedicated to growth and self-edification. Married for thirteen years, Tracee divorced in 2015 and began a new journey. The challenges of divorce and coparenting as a single woman have elevated her spiritual, personal, professional, and entrepreneurial paths. Tracee remarried in 2022 and with her husband, Etoya White, launched Aligned Faith Coaching. Together, they have aligned their faith and their passion to help people become the best versions of themselves and have the healthiest possible relationships. In 2023 Tracee also became a published author with her first anthology project, *Behind the Desk*.

Stephanie Malench

From Under the Thumb to Large and In Charge

It is fitting that I am sharing this story in an anthology titled *Perfectly I'mPerfect*, because the roots of my journey are "being perfect" yet never "good enough." The word I heard most growing up was "no."

My whole life, I have been a perfectionist. I wanted perfect grades, perfect health, and a perfect relationship with a man. I was the teacher's helper all through school, grading papers, helping other students, even pulling their loose teeth. I did everything I could to avoid getting in trouble, was embarrassed if my name got put on the board (back in the dark ages when it was done in chalk), and wouldn't tell my parents (again, back in the dark ages when behavior sheets weren't sent home for parents to sign).

Being in trouble at school didn't happen often—only twice that I remember. In kindergarten, I got in trouble because I left circle time to go sit on the edge of a table. I needed to pull up my knee socks but didn't have room to stretch out my legs. So I imitated my teacher, who often sat on the table edge pulling up her stockings. My other "I'm in trouble" moment was in third grade because I spoke to the classmate next to me while we had a guest speaker. I was certain my parents would learn of this transgression because the speaker was friends with my high-school-aged sister!

Because my father was a doctor, I was under pressure to get good grades, and not *just* good, but excellent. That wasn't difficult in grade school and junior high because extra credit was available. If I didn't have *more than* 100 percent in a class, I felt I was slacking.

I loved learning, so this effort was fun. My love for doing extra work even went beyond completing work for extra credit. I took the vocabulary tests at the back of the giant World Book Dictionary and, throughout elementary school, bought workbooks for grammar and math that were two or three grade levels ahead of me, completing them in a week.

Although I was getting good grades, my parents wouldn't allow me to join the gifted pull-out program in fifth or sixth grade. Then, in junior high and high school, the work got tougher. Because I had excellent grades, I was placed in all advanced classes with students from the other schools in my district. I discovered that they had moved through a more rigorous curriculum (before everything was standardized statewide).

I struggled with the math classes and was making consistent Cs and Ds (in my family, a C was considered an F because you "didn't try"). Tutoring services were not readily available at that time, and my siblings were all out of the house and away at college. So instead of getting the help I needed to succeed at a higher level, I had to move down to the "average" math classes. I felt like a failure, even though I started making As and Bs again.

This family drive for perfectionism also showed painfully in my body image. In fourth grade, at the ripe old age of ten, I was already reading health magazines on my own initiative, believing I had been overweight for years. When other kids my age were eating cheeseburgers and chicken nuggets at restaurants, I was ordering the largest veggie salad or veggie sandwich on the menu and getting told by my parents that I was eating too much. Yet Mom mainly made Hamburger Helper at home, with me as an "only child" and my siblings all away at college.

Stephanie Malench | From Under the Thumb to Large and In Charge

My diet at home got worse as I got older because Mom was tired of being a mom. Yet, my dad and I were not allowed to cook. My senior year in high school, my mom began body-shaming me at a new level. For example, she squeezed my hand as we walked through the mall behind a large-bodied woman and asked me, loudly enough for the woman to hear, if I wanted to grow up to look like that. Around this time, doctors discovered some endocrine imbalances resulting in weight gain and growth of body hair. Great, I thought, I will be fat and hairy. I believed I truly was physically ugly.

I was a tomboy in these younger years and loved to play soccer during recess with the boys. So, naturally, when I got to high school, I wanted to try out for the soccer team. Even though my brother and one of my other sisters were in athletics in high school, my parents told me no because I was fat and was already getting made fun of and called names frequently in school.

Without athletics, even my numerous other service groups and clubs didn't make me eligible for the National Honor Society. My parents did not allow me to apply for college scholarships or to be recognized for my good grades because "we didn't need the money." To this day, I have never been recognized for or received an award for any of my achievements: academic, volunteer, or professional.

Living at home while in college continued poor trends in my diet. Mom refused to make anything. She and I went out for lunch, and because my dad's office catered breakfasts and lunches for employees, Dad brought home fast food for dinner. Mom put herself and dad on the same diet I was on, even though my mom was already underweight.

My parents also viewed as failures the events of my dating life. When no guy had asked me out yet, I took the initiative during my junior year in high school. I flirted with a boy from my honors classes, who was also on the football team and had older siblings the same ages as mine. Every holiday, I bought sweetheart grams from student council fundraising to be delivered to him. A teacher who liked me helped me by giving him anonymous bouquets of red and white balloons and other treats every day of Valentine's Day week. I even walked with him to his locker, hoping for a kiss between classes.

A few weeks later, my dad found out his mom had terminal cancer. My mom blamed it on me for stressing her out because her son didn't like me.

My senior year in high school I tried flirting with the college boys who worked at the YMCA. I was there working out as part of the "I-need-to-get-my-stomach-strong-to-get-a-tummy-tuck" routine Mom had designed for me after I'd lost nearly sixty pounds the previous summer. I didn't like the Nautilus machines and started having these guys teach me and spot me doing free weights.

My sophomore year in college I had three failed attempts to have a relationship with a guy, all ending with calls to my mom from theirs. My parents told me I was an embarrassment to them, as they were well known in my community. It got so bad one night, I tried to strangle myself with my bed sheet.

Not long after I graduated from grad school, my mom died suddenly from a massive heart attack. The physical cleanup from my mom's severe depression and hoarding disorder began. Twenty-five years' worth of outgrown or never-worn clothes, magazines, piles of plastic bags, my toys that I had boxed and bagged up in fourth grade for Goodwill…all finally left the house in just two days.

The realization that my experiences as a child and young adult were not the result of "overprotective" parenting, but emotional and mental abuse, finally occurred in 2020. I met someone though my job who became a wonderful friend and mentor who believed in me, built me up, and has been my biggest cheerleader for the past three years. He has taught me that it is OK to ask for respect from employers and coworkers, and encouraged me to ask for a raise. After a lifetime of being told I could do nothing, he tells me I can do anything.

After years of being told to "not make waves," I have made a tsunami! I ran for mayor of my hometown (even though I lost, my mentor was proud of me for my courage) and asked for a raise for the first time in 2021. In 2022, I left my full-time job after giving the required two-week notice, even though my boss asked me to stay until my replacement was hired so I could train them. I also recently walked away from a $35,000+ per year contract because the business owner was constantly putting me down and treating me in a negative manner.

Standing up for myself and not being afraid of what "might" happen feels good! I look to the future much more than I look to the past. Sometimes it just takes one special person to believe in you and your life is changed forever.

Everyone who has known me well has seen the change in my self-confidence and attitude. Of course, not everyone encouraged the change, because I have stopped being a people pleaser. I know it is OK to make mistakes, and I can now say to others, when it's right to do so, what was over-said to me for all those years of childhood: No!

Stephanie Malench is an accomplished author and now runs her own full-service writing and editing business, Write By Steph. Her books include *The ABCs of Living Independently When You are Older or Frail, 2nd Edition,* and *The Ultimate Beginner's Guide to Clean Living.* When she is not working (which isn't often, because she loves her job), Stephanie enjoys going to museums, antique stores, and cooking. Her home is a revolving door for foster cats, and she has one of her own, Ginger, who was previously her father's.

Terri Schneider

New Beginnings

One of the beautiful things about life is that *you* have the power to change it! Change is hard; it's messy. You may even lose a few people along the way, but it's something for which you will thank your future self!

Just before turning forty, I found myself at a crossroads. I had been living my life by just going through the motions of what I thought I was supposed to do. I was a wife and a mom who did everything she could to make everyone happy, but it still never seemed to be enough. I married my high school sweetheart, had two beautiful children, and a home. Life was grand, or at least I thought it should be.

I always worked but never made a lot money. My husband was the breadwinner and constantly reminded me I wouldn't have anything if it wasn't for him. I believed that wholeheartedly, as I'd grown up in poverty. My dad passed away when I was two, and my mom did everything she could to provide for my sister and me. Our home was full of love, but we sometimes lacked the bare necessities. (I ate a lot of mayonnaise and cheese sandwiches growing up!) My husband was obviously right: I wouldn't have anything if it wasn't for him. I should feel so lucky that I had a job, a home, and a family…what else did I need?

After her battle with kidney failure, I lost my mom, best friend, and the only person who has shown me unconditional love. She said something to me before she passed that hit me to the core: "It's not about the quantity of life, it's about the quality of life!" These words made me start thinking deeply about my life and what I wanted. I have one life to live, and so far I have lived it trying to make everyone else happy!

Thanks to Mom's wisdom, I started working on myself. I asked myself, Who am I, what do I like to do, what do I want to do, and how do I want to be treated? The more I tried to answer those questions, the more I felt lost and depressed. I started going to counseling. The more I tried to heal myself and figure myself out, the worse my marriage got. We never had a perfect marriage, but I felt the more I tried to work on me, the worse it got.

We argued about everything, and I felt I could never do anything right. It seemed as though I couldn't say anything about the way I was feeling without being labeled crazy, because only crazy people go to counseling. I was criticized for crying because only babies cry. I found myself hiding in my closet, even locking myself in the laundry room or my car, just to cry safely.

Eventually the verbal arguments turned physical. First behind closed doors, then in front of the kids, and eventually in public. When I tried to remove myself from the situations, it only made matters worse. I landed at the doctor's office with a pulled ligament in my hand, after he dragged me out of my car when I tried to leave. Other times I would find myself blocked in my driveway by family members adding to my husband's efforts to control me: *the grass isn't greener on the other side, you don't want to leave everything you have, you won't be able to take the kids with you.* They even threatened that attorneys in their family would make sure I wouldn't get child custody.

I felt helpless. I believed every word. *They are right. I don't have anywhere I can go. I don't have parents I can go to. My sister lives in another state, and I can't uproot my children's world. My friends are his friends, and*

I can't put them in the middle of this. I can't afford to live on my own. I won't leave my kids. All these negative thoughts circled through my mind like a hurricane. It seemed that staying in that life was my only choice. I was stuck with nowhere to go. I felt hopeless, numb. This living hell was going to be the rest of my life.

One morning, I called in sick to work after a long night of arguments; it was a common occurrence after he spent the evening hours at the bar. When he woke up, he asked me why I wasn't at work and if I was OK. I asked if he remembered last night, and he said he didn't. In that moment I knew I couldn't do it anymore. I couldn't continue to be a target of abuse and the only one to remember what was going on.

Together, we crafted a plan to separate. I took on the work of figuring out where I would go and how everything would work. We would separate after Christmas to give the kids that bit of normalcy.

We made an appointment with a mediator. We start talking about everything we wanted to see in the separation, and then I heard, "Can I date other people while we are separated? I want to start dating immediately." I sat there with my mind racing in a million directions. *We're here to separate so we can work on ourselves, to see if we can save our marriage... I thought we were going to see if we could get along better after being separated for a while...How can he want to date other people? He really doesn't love me...I can't stay married to someone who wants to date other people...*

Then, I said it. The words came out of my mouth, "Why are we here talking about a separation if you want to immediately start dating other people? If you want to date other people, I want a divorce, not a separation!"

In that moment, I felt broken, scared, relieved, sad, and happy, all at the same time.

And so I found myself restarting my life at forty. When I left him, I took only my personal belongings, my family sentimental items, a dresser, and two chairs. I rented a house in our town. I didn't have beds for us to sleep on, a couch to sit on, a table to eat at, or everyday necessities.

My family and friends rallied around me. They pitched in to buy a bed for each of my girls. My sister took me shopping and bought me some household necessities. Even though I was scared I wouldn't be able to afford my bills on my own, I financed the rest of the furniture so I could give my girls a normal home.

New beginnings can be fun and exciting, but they can also be full of fear and darkness. I had been so out of touch with my feelings for so long that I didn't know what to do with all of them. The comfort of numbing the emotions was a familiar path from those years of emotional abuse, and so I started drinking them away. I was going out a lot, drinking, and seeking attention from anyone who would give it to me. Then the pandemic hit, and the world shut down. I found myself at home, drinking alone, just so I wouldn't have to feel all these emotions.

I knew this wasn't the person I wanted to be. I had to use considerable force of will just to be in my own thoughts. Being alone with your thoughts can be a scary and dark place! Some emotions were really hard to get through. *I know it was best for me to leave, so why do I feel guilty? Why do I feel sad about it? At the same time, I'm guilty and sad, why am I angry at myself for staying as long as I did? And why* did *I stay for as long as I did?*

It took me a long time to figure out that I was in mourning. That life was the only life I had known for twenty-three years. I left a home that I had put my heart and soul into. I left our dog; I left all the rooms in which I made so many good memories with my girlies. I stayed for as long as I did because I thought it was best for everyone, but I was wrong. It was the worst thing, and for that I was angry with myself. If I had left sooner, I could have saved us from some of the pain we'd faced. I stayed because I was scared. I was scared I would lose my kids; I was scared I wouldn't be able to do it by myself; I was scared to lose friends; I was scared to be alone.

I have learned so much through this process. I must take time to sit in my thoughts, as scary as it is sometimes. Now I know that even in hardship, I can keep pursuing a dream, and I know that I am worthy to be on this earth. I have learned that I am something, for I have seen what I am truly capable of. Now I see the truth that it's never too late to try something new. I know that people come and go out of my life, but true friends and family will be there for me in my darkest times. I have learned my self-worth, that I am the only one in control of my life, and that only I have the power to change it! For all of those learnings, I am truly thankful!

Through this major life transition, my dream of becoming a financial advisor has come true, and I became a homeowner again, *by myself*, making new, beautiful memories with my girlies! Don't let other people's words limit your beliefs; you are capable of amazing things!

Here's to *your* future self, and cheers to New Beginnings!

Terri Schneider is a financial advisor dedicated to empowering individuals and businesses to achieve their financial success and confidence. With more than eighteen years of experience in the financial services industry, Terri is known for her personal attention, and for her commitment to her clients' best interests. In this role, Terri is committed to building long-lasting relationships built on trust, integrity, and open communication. She takes time to listen to her clients' needs, objectives, and concerns, to help ensure that she delivers personalized financial solutions that align with their financial goals. Her passion has been to make a positive impact on others' lives. When she is not in the office, you can find her volunteering or fundraising for various organizations throughout the community, cheering on the St. Louis Cardinals, and being her daughters' biggest cheerleader!

Tonya Winingar

How the Hell Did I Do THAT?

Each of us authors is an ordinary woman overcoming the extraordinary. Sadly, I know that my story of overcoming is all too ordinary. I'm not going to talk about the details of my abuse. I don't need to; most women have known some kind of abuse. Mine was diverse and went on for years.

I have a herstory. I did not learn the lessons that my parents were teaching. I learned that the best way to get attention or to receive love was to do acts of service for anyone…*everyone*. I only recently understood my service as self-serving too. I served because I wanted others to see me, give me praise, love me.

How else did I creatively cope with my abuse…while also creating what would be problems for my adult life? I learned very early that having feelings and expressing them was unsafe. Having feelings got you more of what hurt you. I became a robot. If you cut me, wires poked out and started sparking. So I learned to be careful. Careful with what I said, what I did, how I acted. I stopped crying. From an early age I figured out how to manage other people's anger. Mind-reading big people's faces and body language became how I navigated around them. I became an expert at taking care of other people's feelings so that I wouldn't get hurt. I thought that if I were good enough, smart enough—*perfect*—that adults wouldn't get mad, or drink, or yell.

I have started this chapter in my head every day for weeks. I made several false starts on the keyboard. Each time, I found a distraction to stop myself from getting my thoughts on screen. In fact, I've started the book of my life hundreds of times over a span of years. I even have the outline and chapter titles recorded somewhere. So why am I struggling to "find" the time to sit down and dedicate an hour or so to me and my story?

I ask myself the question, *What really makes me Perfectly I'mPerfect?*

The answer is: Everything. All of it. All at once. I can be a complicated, gentle, raging beast; blunt, stuck, scared by the life inside me, scared by not acting on the passion I have. I have been broken and used, I've healed and been the healer. Trained from early on to be a robot, now I cry—a lot. I worry I will never be enough while at the same time thinking I am too much.

As I tell my story, I worry that there is not enough time left for me to recover. And I know what recovery takes because my profession is counseling; I am a therapist. I help people sort through the s#it in their lives and yet some days can't sort through my own. You know the saying *you can't see the forest for the trees*? It's hard to be objective when you are the subject of your own narrative. As I survived, I also created the coping strategies—like being of service—that are now problems that must be sorted, changed, released.

My biggest learned lesson of all is that the same creativity that got me in my mess will not shift me out of it. My hard-earned advice is: When you can see an unhealthy mental or emotional pattern, like over-helping or being a robot, just go ahead and stop right in the moment. And breathe. And then breathe some more. Then start shifting your thoughts or feelings. And that is so much easier with an emotional-support human. I have seen therapists, coaches, and psychiatrists off and on since I was a teenager.

I have talked about myself so much in those fifty-minute sessions! Many times, the learning boiled down to: I can do this. If I've gotten through "*that*," then I can get through *this*!

I feel strange now when I am not doing an act of service the way I used to. Now, my acts of service are based on my needs. Do I need to do this? What's my motivation? Is this a *kind* thing to do or a *nice* thing to do? My healing process has taught me new lessons. I have learned that perfection does not define a desired, "supposed to be/going to be" future state. Perfect is what *was*, not what it *is* going to be. Huge difference. In fact, I learned to stop being perfect. Which also means that I am not a *nice* person anymore. I am *kind*.

I define a nice person as somebody who keeps the status quo. A nice person tiptoes around on eggshells. A nice person does not acknowledge the elephant in the room. A nice person does their best to navigate around everybody else's needs at the expense of their own.

In my mind, a *kind* person says "F#*K that S*!T!" A kind person does not keep the status quo and knows status quos were meant to be broken. A kind person sees the eggshells on the floor, sees they are broken already, and says, *so why the hell am I gonna tiptoe*? A kind person gets a broom and sweeps that mess right up.

A kind person says, *Excuse me, there is an elephant in the room. How would we like to address this*? I believe a kind person says, "Self comes first; others second." I had to learn to be kind, and I had to do that because my self-preservation depended on it. It's the same principle as on an airplane when the flight attendant tells you to put on your own mask first before helping others. If I am so busy helping other people, then I am not helping myself or *heal*ing myself.

So, the "niceness" of putting the mask on somebody else first, the niceness of keeping the status quo, that niceness of tiptoeing around eggshells so they don't get broken…all that had to stop. My life depended on me being kind, which is acknowledging my limits and setting a boundary, putting myself first. Because when I am taken care of, I am then able to take care.

Being kind to myself allowed me to start using a favorite tool that I teach others, called STOP DROP and ROLL. What this means is that I slow down enough to experience my feelings. I slow down to determine whether I am *reacting* to information or just *acting on* information that is shared with me. This differentiation is one of the most respectful ways I can experience myself, which is to acknowledge both feelings and projections. I get to remember that perception is projection, and that everybody is a mirror for me. I get to feel my feelings and sit with them. I get to name them and have them. What this ultimately means is that I stop taking things personally, and I stop mind-reading and making assumptions. I-ME-MYSELF gets to own my feelings, where they are coming from, and the roles I play in hurting my own feelings.

So what is Perfectly I'mPerfect for me now? It's living in authenticity. It's living in integrity. It's living each day with the knowledge of my values, seeing my worth intrinsic to my core, hearing the caress of my kindness to myself and others, and feeling in alignment with all that I do. I choose to feel and think and hear how I am with the world. I see myself changing so much of how I am able to influence my world and heal. I am no longer skin and wires. I have feelings. And when my eyes leak, I allow myself to call them tears.

As I look back on all that I have done, all that I have lived, I think "how the hell did I do that?" And I see the answer every day, in my grit, determination, tenacity, love, kindness, respect. So many words to describe what I have done and where I have gone. And yet I know I have so much more to learn and so many new ways to grow. Sitting here right now, at 2:56

p.m. on a random Tuesday, I acknowledge that I am a living, breathing embodiment of goals that I had years ago. I am no longer a victim of the abuses that I experienced, and there are still hurts that I am healing. And I am healing. Every day I work with clients, I gain more insight into how to help them and then I sometimes use that nugget to help me. I am nowhere near where I want to be—Yet! And yet I am *so not* where I used to be even a year ago, never mind a decade or thirty years ago. How the Hell Did I Do THAT?? Nah mate, How the Hell can I NOT do more of that?

Tonya Winingar, a compassionate Licensed Professional Counselor and dedicated HEALth Coach, is resolute in her mission to catalyze global healing, transforming lives one individual at a time. Her pioneering HEALth care methodology harmoniously integrates the realms of mind, body, brain, and spirit, empowering individuals to reshape their lives by reshaping their thoughts.

Tonya's holistic approach encompasses a spectrum of modalities including therapy, coaching, neurofeedback, and an unwavering commitment to fostering kindness. Her committed focus is on nurturing those who've weathered trauma, or wrestled with ADD/ADHD, substance-use disorders, depression, and anxiety. Tonya's steadfast commitment lies in guiding people to rediscover their lives, championing holistic well-being at every step.

Traci S. Daniels

The Gift That Keeps on Giving...

I fell to my knees in shock at the news. My breath was shallow; all I could do was grasp my chest as the tears flowed and the shock waves ran throughout my body. Could this be? Was this true? Had I been pregnant more than twenty years ago without knowing it? Did God just answer—with a DNA test—the question buried in my heart for decades?

You never know where a new path will lead. One day, curious about my ancestral origins, I decided to take a DNA test to see how much Native American blood I had flowing through my veins. Both of my parents told me I had Choctaw and Cherokee ancestral roots. I never cared before, but a friend of mine informed me that, with at least 15 percent Native American genes, I would be eligible for financial support from the tribes.

I laugh now as I remember that, indeed, cash was the catalyst for this incredible journey. I proceeded to order the DNA test, and when it arrived I completed the necessary steps, then waited about six weeks for the test to return. When I was notified that my results were in, I first scrolled the app and saw some of my known cousins confirmed as DNA relatives. As I continued to scroll and view all the people with whom I shared DNA, I saw a face that looked mighty familiar. I thought to myself, What in the world is happening here? I know this person is not related to me!

There, listed as related, was my ex-boyfriend, whom I had not seen in more than twenty years! He was not just an ex-boyfriend; he was also my first love. We had been together for two years, so the notion of us being related was more than I could bear. Even though our season had ended and we had moved on, we were still on "social media speaking terms" and remained cordial with one another. So I reached out to him, and the conversation went like this:

Me: "Hey, soooo, I took a DNA test."

Him: "Hey, how are you? Did you find out anything interesting?"

Me: *Silence* (because I was trying to figure out how to say what I just learned)

Him: "Oh, I see, OMG!" (I hadn't realized the DNA company would notify him that we shared DNA.)

Me: "Ummm, what in the world? How are we related? How did we not ever know this?"

Him: "Wow."

Me: "I am speechless."

After some time to process what we had discovered, we began to individually research for a possible ancestral link. Soon, I woke up one morning to a text conversation that turned the world surreal in a moment.

Him: "Hey, Good morning; soooo, I have stumbled upon a potential explanation on why we are showing as DNA matches, which doesn't involve us being related. However, if true, it may be equally unsettling, perhaps..."

Me: "Good morning...Equally unsettling?"

Him: "Yeah, so here goes...Is there a possibility that back in the day, there was an unknown or undetected pregnancy?"

Me: "No, well, anything is possible. However, it wasn't in God's plan for us if it was unknown or undetected."

Him: "I agree, but there is something called fetal microchimerism. In simple terms, it means the transfer of fetal cells (DNA) from the male fetus to the mother during the first weeks of gestation. In miscarriages, those cells can remain for decades or even the life of the mother, and they would be detected in a DNA analysis. I sincerely apologize if any of that was distressing. I can't imagine how it would not be."

Me: "No apology necessary. All is well."

Honestly, I kept my composure as I messaged him; however, I was stressed and completely bewildered! I even googled "How do I extract DNA out of me???" Google was of no help, so I was forced to sit with my emotions and sort them out. I resolved that this result could be an anomaly and that I would take another DNA test from a different company and see what those results would yield.

The following day, I messaged him back.

Me: "Hey. After some great thought, I realized I was completely thrown off by the last theory you presented. However, it could have some validity to it. I decided to order the 23andMe test. I will complete it and see what happens."

Him: "I anticipated that reaction. I spoke to a professional genealogist that I had worked with on another project, and after I disclosed our complete history, she offered this theory, and because the cm number is so high, it is a definite genetic match."

I was left speechless and confused about the many possibilities, but I made up my mind that I was going to trust God and wait patiently on the results.

Weeks later...

Wow. It wasn't an anomaly. Everything in the second DNA test confirmed the first and provided additional information. At this time, I reflected on how I never even knew pregnancy was a possibility for me.

However, according to this information, not only had I been pregnant, but I had been pregnant with a boy.

The reality overtook me, and I fell to my knees, crying. I knew only God knew I carried a profound question, and this was the answer. I had never let those words out of my mouth; I hid them deep in my heart. That's when a cloud of glory encompassed me, and from head to toe I was at peace.

At that very moment, I was made whole. How special am I that God would use a DNA test to reveal this information? Now, I was content knowing that a pregnancy *was* the will of God for my life. I got up from my knees and started to glorify God for the revelation He allowed me to experience. I raised my hands to the heavens with praise in my heart and freedom in my spirit. It was done! Voids were filled that I did not even know existed! It further assured me that God is real, and He knows precisely what we need when we need it.

After more research, I found there are many benefits to this fetal microchimerism phenomenon. In simple terms, it has the potential to extend the life of the mother, acting as a fountain of youth, and has the potential to correct genetic defects within the mother. Past research has shown that microchimerism may even boost immune surveillance, the body's ability to acknowledge and destroy pathogens and cells that might become cancerous. These added cells also play a role in repairing damaged tissue, helping form new blood vessels to heal wounds. Microchimerism is associated with a lower risk of Alzheimer's and breast cancer. These discoveries fascinated me and made me more aware of God's love for me. Not only did the discovery of this once-child fill a void and mend my emotions, but now I had discovered he probably healed my body.

I had always wanted to have children, but it had never come to pass. However, I was content knowing that it was the will of God for my life.

I happen to be a bonus mother to many, and I am grateful that I never struggled with prolonged depression about my apparent inability to have children. However, every Mother's Day, I felt a pang of sadness and would have a moment of weeping.

This year was different. No pangs, no sadness, just pure joy over my baby boy in heaven. In fact, I was a mother. I had been a mother; I just hadn't known.

My child made it to heaven, and that is where I want to go when I leave this earth. I will meet him when I get there, and that was all I desired; that was enough for me. Would I rather I'd met him here on earth? Would I rather have loved his physical form, held him, molded his character, and raised him? Of course. But that wasn't God's plan, and His plan is always perfect. Jeremiah 29:11 says, *"For I know the plans and thoughts that I have for you," says the Lord, "plans for peace and well-being and not for disaster, to give you a future and a hope."* God not only gave me a future and hope, but He gave me this gift of knowledge for this time in my life, and I am grateful. This knowledge of my once-child, this revelation, this boy whose DNA is still within me, is literally the gift that keeps on giving.

Traci S. Daniels is a passionate and charismatic woman of God who serves as the assistant pastor at Anchored in Truth Ministries in Edwardsville, Illinois. A motivational speaker, she is the Founder and CEO of women-revive.com. Traci also serves as the president of her local NAACP branch and is an ambassador for the Chamber of Commerce. She serves on several nonprofit boards and is a wife to her wonderful husband. Traci received her Bachelor of Science in Sociology from Southern Illinois University at Edwardsville and is a proud graduate of Jake's Divinity School, powered by North Central University, where she received a Master of Arts in Strategic Leadership. Traci is pursuing a PhD. in Christian Ministry and Leadership at Liberty University. Looking ahead, Traci is on the path to launching her transformational coaching program and practice in the fall of 2023. With her genuine care for people's well-being and her ability to inspire positive change, Traci is poised to impact lives on an even grander scale.

Wendy Edelstein

Home Owned

One random morning in December 2010, a stranger on my doorstep gave me the news I'd been awaiting and dreading—I'd need to be out of my house in three weeks because I'd ceased paying my mortgage some eight months earlier.

This unwanted message capped a five-year chapter that mixed resolve, naivete, joy, disappointment, and resilience. That is to say, I learned a ton. Maybe you, too, have chased a dream with a singular determination? Your dream, like mine, might have represented something aspirational that you hoped would lead to happiness, like mine with home ownership.

My story begins in 2005 when I bought a duplex in Oakland with someone I didn't know, at the height of a Bay Area real-estate frenzy. Low inventory and too many hungry buyers. Everyone understood you had to overbid to be competitive. Back then I worked as a writer in UC Berkeley's Office of Public Affairs. I had just gotten a modest raise and convinced myself I could buy my first home.

It only took a minute to conclude that purchasing an appealing condo on my own in Berkeley or Oakland would be impossible. But then a coworker told me about a friend who had gotten into the market with a TIC, providing me with a ray of hope. "A TIC? What's that?" I asked.

TICs, for anyone who doesn't know the pricey Bay Area, are tenancies-in-common. To get into the real-estate market, you buy a two-unit (or larger) property with someone with whom you have no legal relationship (i.e., not a spouse). Conveniently, the coworker's friend knew a guy named Brian who might be interested.

Soon thereafter, Brian and I met at a wine bar. It wasn't a date in the conventional sense, but we established a fast connection. We laughed a lot that first night. He was the extravert to my introvert, a life of the party guy who lit up a room. A fun guy. I was going to get my home and a new best friend. What could be better?

After a few months of touring houses, Brian discovered a promising property, a 1929 deco-style duplex with side-by-side units in a decent enough Oakland neighborhood. The place looked nautical with its creamy white paint job, dark gray bluish trim, and curved railings. "Ahoy there, maties," it called to us.

Venturing inside, I took in the buttery yellow hardwood plank floors, the view of downtown Oakland, and the abundant natural light. The tiered backyard featured an incense cedar tree, rose bushes, a bricked patio, and a hot tub. A heavenly paradise in urban Oakland. Could this really be happening?

Having toured the house once, Brian showed it to me like a proud parent. I was jittery but decided to go for it. My therapist tried to dissuade me, but I ignored her concerns. What did she know? I was adulting! My parents, with whom I consulted on big life decisions, were conveniently out of the country. We see what we want to see.

I went from liking the house to needing it in thirty-six hours. Brian and I moved quickly, knowing that Bay Area real estate waits for no one. I wrote a "love letter" to the seller promising we would be longtime stewards of the property. We bid $116,000 over the asking price. Yes, $116K. Several days later, we learned that we got the house.

Now we were in it. Brian and I opened a joint checking account and signed a TIC agreement. We bought a large wrought-iron dining table for the patio.

On move-in day, Brian, who worked in tech sales, called to let me know he'd been laid off. No matter. The thrill of getting situated in my new space dulled any concerns. A month later he landed another job. I was in love. House love. Life was very good.

In December, the check for our first property-tax payment bounced. I had placed the necessary funds in our shared account, including the security deposit I'd gotten back from my former landlord. But Brian had deposited too little. He blamed his mistake on the bank. For months. More than a sign, his responses read like a billboard painted with the words "I don't take responsibility for my actions."

I beseeched him repeatedly to look, simply look, at the joint account. This standoff dragged on for months until he conceded his mistake. By then the damage had been done. My trust had splintered. Our friendship, once so promising, was damaged. Irrevocably, it would turn out.

We went from a budding friendship to combatants, polarized on nearly every household decision. Being a homeowner was much more complicated and expensive than I'd reckoned. So, when the ancient hot tub broke down annually, requiring hundreds of dollars in parts, I balked at immediately repairing it. Brian, who used it to seduce guys, insisted.

Brian would lose jobs twice more over the next four years. The last time was early 2009 when the economy soured. We refinanced our loan to hold onto the house. By early 2010 he had been out of work for a year. The life of the party guy no longer entertained or went out.

On January 17, 2010, a Sunday, I got a call from the woman who had introduced us. Brian had been found dead in a local park. A suicide. I was shocked but not surprised.

That day marked the beginning of what a friend later dubbed my "horribilis annus." My horrible year. I became determined to hold onto my home despite Brian's death. I turned to our TIC agreement, but nowhere did the boilerplate document stipulate what would happen in the event of an owner's death. I consulted with our realtor. She was no help.

I lived and breathed my dilemma. I was in uncharted territory and tapped anyone and everyone I knew to help. In the years since purchasing the property, the bottom of the real estate market had collapsed. I owed more on the place than it was worth.

My parents wanted me to bail and walk away. The same stubbornness that got me into the mess in the first place kept me dug in and committed to my cause. Was it a losing one? I didn't know, but I was determined to unearth every option. A tennis friend and real-estate attorney put me in touch with a colleague who gave generously of her time and expertise.

To make matters worse, I learned just three months later in March that my job of six years was in jeopardy. I'd faced adversity before, but this two-pronged assault was something new.

My real-estate attorney advised me on how to work with the banks holding the property's two loans. She told me that they wouldn't take me seriously in my need to adjust my loan terms until I stopped paying. So that's what I did in hopes that would lead to a negotiation.

Meanwhile, I knew my time at my job was coming to an end. The department's Human Resources rep was calling me in for conversations. Of course, she was not concerned with my well-being. My work, which my former manager had deemed sufficient and sometimes excellent, went downhill as I was given assignments that were well out of my comfort zone.

When my doorbell rang that random December 2010 morning, I knew I'd be losing the property. The bank offered me "cash for keys," provided I left the place spotless after departing.

A week later, I resigned from my job, ensuring my record at the university wouldn't be marred by a dismissal. I had loved that job and the smart, funny colleagues in my department. But I knew that I was done.

During the three weeks the bank gave me to move out, I had time to think while I cleaned, packed, and began searching for my next home. Though I still loved my house, it no longer felt like mine. I consoled myself knowing that I had done everything in my power to keep it.

I knew I'd been horribly, wonderfully stubborn in my efforts to hang onto the house. Rather than second-guess myself, I felt resilient and strong. I reasoned that I fought for the house because it was my dream and, of the two dramas playing out in my life, it was the one that felt less personal.

As I navigated those final weeks in the house, I felt proud of my grit. Friends came to help me pack. At the eleventh hour, I'd managed to land a sweet rental on a beautiful North Berkeley street, which felt like a miracle. I remember packing up my books and reflecting on what I knew to be true—the people I loved would still be in my life after I left my house. I had my health. I'd be OK.

Wendy Edelstein's recovery from her 2010 *horribilis annus* didn't end with this story's end. After finding a place to live, she needed a new job, but her professional self-confidence was low. She decided to pivot, and trained as a coach so that she could use her intuition and pursue her love of personal development. In 2014 she established Changeover Coaching, LLC. Wendy now works as an executive and leadership coach, and supports leaders to elevate their communication skills, navigate complexity, and boost their impact.

In 2021, Wendy left the San Francisco Bay Area and moved to St. Louis, Missouri, where she had grown up, to be near her family. She now lives in a condo she can call her own with her two cats, Carl and Roger.

ACKNOWLEDGEMENTS

This book is dedicated to my husband Billy who supports me like no other, to my children Will & Anna whom I love to the moon and back, to my parents who have kept me grounded and loved me unconditionally, to my tribe who has always had my back, to my soul sisters who helped me find my superpower, to the amazing contributing authors who linked arms with me to allow our stories to become a survival guide for others, and to all the numerous dragonflies that have appeared throughout my life, you have all played an instrumental part in allowing me to pick up the pieces when at times life seemed to be falling apart. Thank you all for loving me through the messy.

Love,
Me
Mom
Your favorite daughter
Scorpion
Tara

To My Beloved Family, My Tribe, My Soul Sisters, and Fellow Authors,

As I embark on this journey through the pages of this book, I am overwhelmed with gratitude and a profound sense of connection to each of you. This dedication is a humble attempt to express the depth of my appreciation for your unwavering support, love, and companionship throughout my life, our season together and this project.

To My Beautiful Family; my husband Michael and my children; Kayla, Patrick, Sydney & Elijah,

You are the bedrock of my existence, the roots from which I draw my strength, and the endless source of love that sustains me. Through all the ups and downs, you have stood by me with unwavering faith. Your encouragement, sacrifices, and boundless love have been the guiding light on my path. This book is a testament to the values, wisdom, and resilience you help nurture within me. Thank you for always believing in me. I love you beyond measure!

continued on next page

To My Tribe,

You are the extended family I chose, a diverse tapestry of friendships and connections that enrich my life beyond measure. Together, we have shared laughter and tears, celebrated victories, and weathered storms. Your presence has added color to the canvas of my existence, and your collective wisdom has expanded my horizons. This book reflects our shared experiences and the lessons we've learned together. Thank you for being my tribe, my chosen family.

To My Soul Sisters,

You are the kindred spirits who have touched the deepest recesses of my heart. Through the tapestry of time, our souls found one another, and our bonds have grown stronger with each passing day. Your unwavering support, empathy, and shared dreams have been a constant source of inspiration. This book is a tribute to the sisterhood we share and the strength it imparts. Thank you for being the sisters of my soul, for always having my back and for calling me out when it is necessary.

To My Fellow Authors,

You are my comrades in arms, the scribes who've shared this arduous yet beautiful path of crafting words. Your willingness, vulnerability, and the countless discussions about the art of writing have changed me in ways I never thought possible. This book is a reflection of the community we've built together, united by our love for empowering others. Thank you for being fellow visionaries who chose to walk beside me, I am forever grateful.

In dedicating this book to all of you, I acknowledge that it would not have been possible without your love, encouragement, and unwavering belief in me. As you turn the pages of this book, know that each word is a reflection of the love and gratitude I hold in my heart for each and every one of you. We all at times, pick up the pieces and put ourselves back together to become something more unique and beautiful than we were before.

With all my love,
Nina & Mom

Made in the USA
Monee, IL
09 October 2023

44303335R00144